crocheted squares

celebration and nature-inspired blocks for garlands and greetings cards, plus stunning projects

kate eastwood

CICO BOOKS

To all my fellow crocheters around the world who know the sheer joy of picking up a simple crochet hook and a ball of yarn. No more words needed.

Published in 2025 by CICO Books
an imprint of Ryland Peters & Small Ltd
20–21 Jockey's Fields, London WC1R 4BW
www.rylandpeters.com
Email: euregulations@rylandpeters.com

10 9 8 7 6 5 4 3 2 1

Text © Kate Eastwood 2025
Design, illustration and photography
© CICO Books 2025

The designs in this book are copyright and must not be crocheted for sale.

The author's moral rights have been asserted. All rights reserved. No part of this publication may be reproduced, stored in a retrieval system, or transmitted in any form or by any means, electronic, mechanical, photocopying, or otherwise, without the prior permission of the publisher.

A CIP catalogue record for this book is available from the British Library.

ISBN: 978 1 80065 464 8

Printed in China

Editor: Marie Clayton
Pattern checker: Jemima Bicknell
Designer: Alison Fenton
Photographer: James Gardiner
Stylist: Nel Haynes
Illustrator: Stephen Dew

In-house editor: Jenny Dye
Art director: Sally Powell
Creative director: Leslie Harrington
Production manager: Gordana Simakovic
Publishing manager: Carmel Edmonds

The authorised representative in the EEA is Authorised Rep Compliance Ltd., Ground Floor, 71 Lower Baggot Street, Dublin, D01 P593, Ireland
www.arccompliance.com

contents

Introduction 4

chapter 1
seasonal squares 6

Spring blossom wreath 8
Spring snowdrops 11
Summer beehive and foxgloves 14
Summer meadow 17
Autumn wreath 20
Autumn hedgehog with toadstool umbrella 23
Winter mistletoe sprig 26
Winter penguin 29

chapter 2
greetings squares 32

Wedding car 34
Wedding cake 37
Valentine's bouquet 40
Valentine's heart 42
New home cottage scene 45
New home front door 48
Birthday present 50
Birthday cupcake 52
Baby's pram 54
New baby in a basket 57

chapter 3
celebration squares 60

Easter rabbit 62
Easter nest 65
Diwali candle 68
Hanukkah candelabra 71
Christmas wreath 74
Christmas tree 76
Christmas letter box and presents 79

chapter 4
projects 82

Tutti-frutti blanket 84
Square tissue box cover 87
Gingham baby blanket 90
Chunky bobbly cushions 92
Bobbly grab bag 95
Chequered place mats and coasters 98
Daisy-and-dot hot water bottle cover 101
Autumn garland 104
Seasonal tree picture 110
Christmas card 113

How to use and display the picture squares 116   Techniques 117
Suppliers 127   Crochet stitch conversion chart, acknowledgements and index 128

introduction

Welcome to my collection of crocheted squares! When coming up with the idea for this book I very much wanted to take the simple crocheted granny square a little further. Squares are often the start of everyone's crochet journey, so I wanted to look at ways that squares can be used for other projects as well as everyone's favourite go-to of a blanket.

The projects in this book are divided into two sections, and the first section includes three chapters with the themes of seasons, greetings and celebrations. Each square base is worked as simple rows of double crochet and then pictures are added by working separate crochet pieces that are stitched onto the squares.

The second section of patterns are larger projects where crochet squares are an integral part of the design, but rather than squares worked in a round, the crochet is worked in rows. In this chapter you will find patterns such as a colourful bobbly grab bag, a gingham baby blanket, a tissue box cover made up of five squares and a bright and cheerful patchwork blanket with squares worked in different crochet stitches.

The idea with the small picture squares is that they can be used for a variety of different makes such as wall art, greetings cards, collages and garlands (see page 116 for ideas and tips). It's entirely up to you! And, because each square uses a very small amount of yarn, they will help you to work your way through that ever-increasing yarn stash!

The Seasonal Squares mark the changing seasons of the year, and they are perfect for putting into small box picture frames or larger collage frames. A collection of four wreaths for the four seasons in a box frame would make a beautiful and unique handmade gift. If garlands are more your thing, why not string together a selection of squares working through from spring to winter.

The Greetings Squares chapter is probably my favourite part of the book as they were so much fun to design. Rather than spending money on a greetings card, what could be more special than making a handmade one? From wedding days to new babies and birthdays to new homes, these squares have got you covered for every occasion.

The Celebration Squares include pictures that celebrate Easter, Hanukkah, Christmas and Diwali. Each square works up to be the perfect size to attach to a blank greeting card and to be popped in the post or posted through a door.

I very much hope that this will become a book that you can dip into for ideas and inspiration, leading you to create many projects and designs of your own.

BEFORE YOU BEGIN

If you are new to crochet, turn to the Techniques section on pages 117–127 and the Abbreviations on page 127. Each project has a skill rating, from Easy (one circle) to Intermediate (two circles) and Advanced (three circles). Start with the Easy patterns then move on to the next two levels once you know the basic techniques.

GENERAL PATTERN NOTES
Yarn
For all the patterns for the squares I have given the yarn brand, colour and weight. Since all the squares are small I have not given an exact quantity for each colour, because only small amounts of each yarn are required, which makes all of these projects perfect for using up leftover yarn. If you are using the same yarns as the pattern, the maximum amount you will need of any colour will be one ball.

Throughout, the main yarn used for the motifs is Cascade Heritage 4-ply because it has a large range of colours in both 4-ply (fingering) and DK (light worsted), which you could use instead of 4-ply (see Tension, opposite). For the motifs I have only listed the colours rather than labelling them as A, B and so on. The two that are the exceptions to this are the Christmas tree and Christmas wreath, because they use several different shades of green which were easier to identify with letters.

Tension (gauge)
This has not been included for the square patterns because each project is small and tension is not particularly significant.

I have given approximate finished measurements for each square but this will vary slightly if you are using leftover yarns and they are of a different yarn weight to the ones I have used. Where I have used 4-ply (fingering) yarn, DK (light worsted) will work equally well – the square will just be a little larger. Similarly, if 4-ply is used where I have used DK, the finished square will work out a little bit smaller. If you are using a different weight yarn to the one in the pattern you may need to size up or down on the crochet hook size. This will not matter but will simply make the finished item a tiny bit larger or smaller.

Finishing the background square
Blocking your finished squares (see page 123) will make all the difference to your work. If your square is not regularly shaped, blocking will enable you to create a perfect square.

Adding motifs to the background square
For each square I have detailed how the individual pieces are attached to the finished square, either by stitching them on with a sewing needle and thread or sticking them on using a hot glue gun. When adding smaller pieces, such as attaching leaves to the wreaths, I found a pair of tweezers to be very helpful. I also found it useful to have a pack of water-soluble coloured pencils to add shade and colour where needed. Once made very slightly wet, the pencil works like a watercolour paint on the yarn.

TIP
For a neat bottom edge to each square, rather than working the first row into the front of the initial chain, tilt the chain slightly towards you – you will see bumps at the back of the chain (see page 118). By working into the bumps instead of the front of the chain you will create a more solid, neater starting edge.

chapter 1
seasonal squares

Nothing is more joyful than the arrival of spring blossom and this miniature wreath allows you to bring that taste of spring inside. The blossom flowers really could not be simpler to make, being just one round of stitches worked in a magic ring, while the centres are just a dot of colour from a coloured pencil.

spring blossom wreath

SKILL RATING ● ○ ○

YARN AND MATERIALS

FOR THE BACKGROUND SQUARE:
Rowan Summerlite 4 ply (100% cotton), 4-ply (fingering) weight, 175m (191yd) per 50g (1¾oz) ball
 1 ball of Mint shade 451 (light green) (A)
 Small amount of Mustard shade 455 (yellow) (B)

FOR THE WREATH:
Cascade Heritage (75% wool, 25% nylon), 4-ply (fingering) weight, 400m (437yd) per 100g (3½oz) skein (hank)
 Small amounts of:
 White shade 5682
 Herb shade 5658 (green)

Rowan Summerlite 4 ply (100% cotton), 4-ply (fingering) weight, 175m (191yd) per 50g (1¾oz) ball
 Small amount of Mustard shade 455 (yellow) (B)

Wired paper cord/thick string

Small twigs (optional)

HOOK AND EQUIPMENT

3mm (US D) crochet hook

2.5mm (US B-1 to C-2) crochet hook

2mm (US steel size 4) crochet hook

Yarn needle

Blocking pins and mat

Pink water-soluble coloured pencil for blossom centres

Hot glue gun

TENSION (GAUGE)
Exact tension is not important for this project.

FINISHED MEASUREMENTS
9.5 x 9.5cm (3¾ x 3¾in)

ABBREVIATIONS
See page 127.

BACKGROUND SQUARE

Using a 3mm (US D) hook and A, ch23.
Row 1: Starting in second ch from hook, 1dc in back bump of each ch to end, turn. (*22 sts*)
Row 2: Ch1 (does not count as st), 1dc in each st, turn.
Rows 3–22: Rep Row 2.
Fasten off.

Edging

Round 1: Using a 2.5mm (US B-1 to C-2) hook and A, with RS facing join in yarn at centre bottom of square with a sl st, 1dc in same st, *1dc in each st to corner, 3dc in corner st, 1dc in each row-end to next corner, 3dc in corner st; rep from * once more, 1dc in each st to beg of round, sl st to join.
Fasten off and sew in ends (see page 123).
Round 2: With RS facing, join B at centre bottom with a sl stBLO, *ch2, sl stBLO in each of next 2 sts; rep from * to beg of round, sl st to join.
Fasten off and sew in ends.

spring blossom wreath

WREATH BASE
Take a long length of wired paper cord or thick string and wind several circles on top of each other to get the required thickness for your wreath base, approx. 1cm (3/8in). Wind a second length of wired paper cord/string around the circles to secure in place as one thick circle.

BLOSSOM
(make 21)
Using a 2mm (US steel size 4) hook and White, make a magic ring.
Round 1: Ch1, [2htr, sl st] 3 times into ring, sl st to join. (*3 petals*)
Fasten off.

LEAVES
(make 11 in Herb, 9 in Mustard)
Using a 2mm (US steel size 4) hook, ch4.
Round 1: Starting in second ch from hook, sl st in next ch, 1dc in next ch, sl st in next ch.
Fasten off.

FINISHING
Block the square (see page 123).
    Slightly dampen the tip of a pink water-soluble coloured pencil and make a small dot in the centre of each blossom.
    Use a hot glue gun to stick the wreath base in the centre of the square.
    Start by sticking the small twigs around the wreath, then stick on the blossoms and add the leaves in between.

At just 7cm (2¾in) tall this little flower pot of freshly sprung snowdrops will bring all the hope that comes with the arrival of spring. Each tiny flower has a wire stem so that the flowers can be arranged to give a 3-D effect to the finished square. A touch of moss and a weathered finished on the terracotta pot add the final details.

spring snowdrops

SKILL RATING ● ○ ○

YARN AND MATERIALS

FOR THE BACKGROUND SQUARE:
Rowan Summerlite 4 ply (100% cotton), 4-ply (fingering) weight, 175m (191yd) per 50g (1¾oz) ball
- 1 ball of Mint shade 451 (light green) (A)
- Small amount of Mustard shade 455 (yellow) (B)

FOR THE SNOWDROP AND POT:
Cascade Heritage (75% wool, 25% nylon), 4-ply (fingering) weight, 400m (437yd) per 100g (3½oz) skein (hank)
- Small amounts of:
- Cinnamon shade 5640 (reddish brown)
- White shade 5682
- Cedar Green shade 5684 (dark green)

A few stems of 26-gauge florist's wire in dark green

Small amount of dried moss

HOOK AND EQUIPMENT
3mm (US D) crochet hook
2.5mm (US B-1 to C-2) crochet hook
2mm (US steel size 4) crochet hook
Yarn needle
Blocking pins and mat
Spray starch
Water-soluble coloured pencils for aging pot
Sewing needle and thread
Scissors to cut wire
Hot glue gun

TENSION (GAUGE)
Exact tension is not important for this project.

FINISHED MEASUREMENTS
9.5 x 9.5cm (3¾ x 3¾in)

ABBREVIATIONS
See page 127.

BACKGROUND SQUARE
Using a 3mm (US D) hook and A, ch23.
Row 1: Starting in second ch from hook, 1dc in back bump of each ch to end, turn. (*22 sts*)
Row 2: Ch1 (does not count as st), 1dc in each st, turn.
Rows 3–22: Rep Row 2.
Fasten off.

Edging
Round 1: Using a 2.5mm (US B-1 to C-2) hook and A, with RS facing join in yarn at centre bottom of square with a sl st, 1dc in same st, *1dc in each st to corner, 3dc in corner st, 1dc in each row-end to next corner, 3dc in corner st; rep from * once more, 1dc in each st to beg of round, sl st to join. Fasten off and sew in ends (see page 123).
Round 2: With RS facing, join B at centre bottom with a sl stBLO, *ch2, sl stBLO in each of next 2 sts; rep from * to beg of round, sl st to join.
Fasten off and sew in ends.

FLOWER POT
Use 2 strands of Cinnamon held together throughout.
Using a 2.5mm (US B-1 to C-2) hook and 2 strands of Cinnamon held together, make a magic ring.
Row 1: Ch1 (does not count as st throughout), (sl st, 1dc, 1htr, 1dc, sl st) into ring. (*5 sts*)

Gently close ring to form a semi-circle, turn.
Row 2: Ch1, 1dc in each st, turn.
Row 3: Ch1, 2dc in first st, 1dc in each st to last st, 2dc in last st. (7 *sts*)
Fasten off.
Row 4: With RS facing, join 2 strands of Cinnamon at start of Row 3, 1dcBLO in each st, turn. (7 *sts*)
Rows 5 and 6: Ch1, 1dc in each st, turn.
Row 7: Ch1, 2dc in first st, 1dc in each st to last st, 2dc in last st, turn. (9 *sts*)
Rows 8–10: Ch1, 1dc in each st, turn.
Row 11: Ch1, 2dc in first st, 1dc in each st to last st, 2dc in last st, turn. (11 *sts*)
Row 12: Ch1, 1dc in each st.
Fasten off.

SNOWDROPS

(make 7)
Using 2mm (US steel size 4) hook and Cedar Green, make a magic ring.
Round 1: 4dc into ring. (4 *sts*)
Fasten off.
Round 2: Join in White, [2dc in next st, 1dc in next st] twice. (6 *sts*)
Rounds 3 and 4: 1dc in each st.
Round 5: [Dc2tog, 1dc in next st] twice. (4 *sts*)
Fasten off, knot White ends and thread yarn tails back down into bud.

BUD LEAVES

(make 7)
Using 2mm (US steel size 4) hook and Cedar Green, ch21.
Row 1: Starting in second ch from hook, sl st in each of next 7 ch, 1dc in each of next 13 ch.
Fasten off.

SINGLE LEAVES

(make 5)
Using 2mm (US steel size 4) hook and Cedar Green, ch21.
Row 1: Starting in second ch from hook, sl st in each ch to end.
Fasten off.

FINISHING

Block the square (see page 123). Block all the leaves and use a spray starch to stiffen.

To 'age' the flower pot, use water-soluble coloured pencils to add shading and give the effect of moss growing on the pot.

Using a sewing needle and thread, stitch the flower pot to the square creating a semi-circle opening at the top as you stitch to allow the buds and leaves to be positioned to give a 3-D effect.

Cut 7 wire stems to a length just slightly longer than needed to fit in the pot. Turn the very tip of one end of each wire over to make a slightly open hook. Now thread the wire, straight end first, through the tip of the bud, bringing it out at the green end. Allow the turned over hook to 'catch' onto the inside of the bud to secure in place. Bend each wire just below the green part of each bulb so that the buds hang down.

Thread a snowdrop bud on the wire through each bud leaf, from front to back, about halfway down the leaf. This allows you to create a leaf 'cap' that sits slightly above each bud.

Arrange the buds and single leaves in the pot and, when you are happy with the positioning, use a hot glue gun to glue the ends securely into the pot.

Use the glue gun to stick a small amount of dried moss around the inside top of the flower pot.

Nothing is more evocative of a summer's day than the sound of bees buzzing around brightly coloured flowers and this little picture square has foxgloves aplenty around the hive for the bees to enjoy. Whether framed as a picture or made into a greetings card, this is a beautiful summer gift.

summer beehive and foxgloves

SKILL RATING ● ● ○

YARN AND MATERIALS

FOR THE BACKGROUND SQUARE:
Rowan Summerlite DK (100% cotton), DK (light worsted) weight, 130m (142yd) per 50g (1¾oz) ball
   1 ball of Pear shade 463 (green) (A)
   Small amount of Pickles shade 475 (golden yellow) (B)

FOR THE HIVE, FLOWERS AND BEES:
Cascade Ultra Pima (100% cotton), DK (light worsted) weight, 200m (220yd) per 100g (3½oz) skein (hank)
   Small amount of Sandstone shade 3828 (light brown)

Cascade Heritage (75% wool, 25% nylon), 4-ply (fingering) weight, 400m (437yd) per 100g (3½oz) skein (hank)
   Small amounts of:
   Charcoal shade 5631 (dark grey)
   Cedar Green shade 5684 (dark green)
   Sage shade 5635 (soft green)
   Herb shade 5658 (green)
   Bordeaux shade 5738 (purple)
   White shade 5682
   Golden Yellow shade 5752 (dark yellow)

Black sewing thread

HOOK AND EQUIPMENT
3mm (US D) crochet hook
2.5mm (US B-1 to C-2) crochet hook
Yarn needle
Blocking pins and mat
Sewing needle and thread

TENSION (GAUGE)
Exact tension is not important for this project.

FINISHED MEASUREMENTS
10 x 10cm (4 x 4in)

ABBREVIATIONS
See page 127.

BACKGROUND SQUARE
Using a 3mm (US D) hook and A, ch23.
Row 1: Starting in second ch from hook, 1dc in back bump of each ch to end, turn. (*22 sts*)
Row 2: Ch1 (does not count as st), 1dc in each st, turn.
Rows 3–22: Rep Row 2.
Fasten off.

Edging
Round 1: Using a 2.5mm (US B-1 to C-2) hook and A, with RS facing join in yarn at centre bottom of square with a sl st, 1dc in same st, *1dc in each st to corner, 3dc in corner st, 1dc in each row-end to next corner, 3dc in corner st; rep from * once more, 1dc in each st to beg of round, sl st to join. Fasten off and sew in ends (see page 123).
Round 2: With RS facing, join B at centre bottom with a sl stBLO, *1dcBLO in next st, ch1, sl stBLO in next st; rep from * to beg of round, sl st to join.
Fasten off and sew in ends.

BEEHIVE
Using a 3mm (US D) hook and Sandstone, ch14.
Row 1: Starting in second ch from hook, 1dc in each ch to end, turn. (*13 sts*)
Rows 2 and 3: Ch1 (does not count as st throughout), 1dcBLO in each st, turn.
Row 4: Ch1, [1dcBLO in each of next 3 sts, dc2togBLO] twice, 1dcBLO in each of next 3 sts, turn. (*11 sts*)

Rows 5 and 6: Ch1, 1dcBLO in each st, turn.
Row 7: Ch1, 1dcBLO in each of next 5 sts, dc2togBLO, 1dcBLO in each of next 4 sts, turn. (*10 sts*)
Rows 8 and 9: Ch1, 1dcBLO in each st, turn.
Row 10: Ch1, 1dcBLO in each of next 2 sts, dc2togBLO, 1dcBLO in each of next 2 sts, dc2togBLO, 1dcBLO in each of next 2 sts, turn. (*8 sts*)
Row 11: Ch1, [dc2togBLO, 1dcBLO in next st] twice, dc2togBLO. (*5 sts*)
Fasten off.
Change to a 2.5mm (US B-1 to C-2) hook, starting at bottom right-hand corner, join in Sandstone with a sl st, 1dc in same st, 1dc in next 9 row-ends, 2dc in next 2 row-ends, 5dc along top edge of hive, 2dc in next 2 row-ends, 1dc in each row-end to bottom of hive.
Fasten off and sew in ends.

FINISHING
Block the square (see page 123).
  Using a sewing needle and thread, stitch the hive to the square creating a slight raised effect to the middle. Using a yarn needle and Sandstone, sew running stitches (see page 126) from the centre top of the hive to the first 'ridge' to create a domed top.
  Using a yarn needle and Charcoal, sew a few stitches at the centre bottom of the hive for the opening.
  Using a yarn needle and Cedar Green or Herb, sew running stitches around the bottom of the hive for grass, then use Sage to sew long straight stitches (see page 126) for the foxglove stems. Using Herb and starting just above the tip of each foxglove stalk, work small French knots (see page 127) for the buds, increasing the knots in size as you work down the stem. Using Bordeaux work slightly bigger French knots beneath the Herb knots. For the foxglove flowers, work two running stitches in Bordeaux next to each other.
  Work some White foxgloves in the same way.
  For the bees, using a yarn needle and Golden Yellow, sew three running stitches on top/adjacent to each other to create a body. Using a sewing needle and black sewing thread stitch a few black rings around the body. Use White to sew a couple of tiny stitches at the top of the body for wings.

Buzzing bees and daisies immediately conjure up images of a lush, green summer meadow, and this tiny square hopes to capture just a snippet of this feeling. Added to a string of summer bunting or made as a gift for a summer birthday present, this square will certainly bring all those summery feelings.

summer meadow

SKILL RATING ● ● ●

YARN AND MATERIALS

FOR THE BACKGROUND SQUARE:
Rowan Summerlite DK (100% cotton), DK (light worsted) weight, 130m (142yd) per 50g (1¾oz) ball
- 1 ball of Pear shade 463 (green) (A)
- Small amount of Pickles shade 475 (golden yellow) (B)

FOR THE FLOWERS AND BEES:
Cascade Heritage (75% wool, 25% nylon), 4-ply (fingering) weight, 400m (437yd) per 100g (3½oz) skein (hank)
- Small amounts of:
  - White shade 5682
  - Mustard shade 5652 (yellow)
  - Lemon shade 5644 (light yellow)
  - Golden Yellow shade 5752 (dark yellow)
  - Herb shade 5658 (green)
  - Cedar Green shade 5684 (dark green)
  - Camel shade 5610 (light brown)
  - Bordeaux shade 5738 (light purple)

Black sewing thread

HOOK AND EQUIPMENT

3mm (US D) crochet hook

2.5mm (US B-1 to C-2) crochet hook

2mm (US steel size 4) crochet hook

Yarn needle

Blocking pins and mat

Sewing needle and thread

TENSION (GAUGE)

Exact tension is not important for this project.

FINISHED MEASUREMENTS

10 x 10cm (4 x 4in)

ABBREVIATIONS

See page 127.

BACKGROUND SQUARE

Using a 3mm (US D) hook and A, ch23.
Row 1: Starting in second ch from hook, 1dc in back bump of each ch to end, turn. *(22 sts)*
Row 2: Ch1 (does not count as st), 1dc in each st, turn.
Rows 3–22: Rep Row 2.
Fasten off.

Edging

Round 1: Using a 2.5mm (US B-1 to C-2) hook and A, with RS facing join in yarn at centre bottom of square with a sl st, 1dc in same st, *1dc in each st to corner, 3dc in corner st, 1dc in each row-end to next corner, 3dc in corner st; rep from * once more, 1dc in each st to beg of round, sl st to join. Fasten off and sew in ends (see page 123).
Round 2: With RS facing, join B at centre bottom with a sl stBLO, *1dcBLO in next st, ch1, sl stBLO in next st; rep from * to beg of round, sl st to join.
Fasten off and sew in ends.

DAISIES

(make 5)
Using a 2.5mm (US B-1 to C-2) hook and White, make a magic ring.
Round 1: *Ch4, starting in second ch from hook, sl st in each of next 3 ch back to magic ring, sl st into ring; rep from * five more times to make 6 petals in total.
Pull up magic ring.
Fasten off and sew in ends.

YELLOW FLOWERS
(make 3)
Using a 2.5mm (US B-1 to C-2) hook and Mustard, make a magic ring.
Round 1: 5dc into ring, sl st in first st to join. (*5 sts*)
Round 2: Ch1 (does not count as st), [2dc in next st] 5 times, sl st to join. (*10 sts*)
Fasten off Mustard.
Round 3: Join Lemon, *(sl stBLO, 1htrBLO, 1trBLO) in next st, (1trBLO, 1htrBLO, sl stBLO) in next st; rep from * four more times to make 5 petals in total, sl st to join. Fasten off and sew in ends.

BEES
(make 2)
Using a 2mm (US steel size 4) hook and Golden Yellow, make a magic ring.
Round 1: 4dc into ring. (*4 sts*)
Round 2: [2dc in next st, 1dc in next st] twice. (*6 sts*)
Rounds 3 and 4: 1dc in each st.
Round 5: [Dc2tog] 3 times. (*3 sts*)
Fasten off and close up opening. Sew in ends.

FINISHING
Block the square (see page 123).

Using a yarn needle and Golden Yellow, work a French knot (see page 127) in the centre of each daisy. Using a sewing needle and thread, stitch the daisies and yellow flowers to the square. Using a yarn needle and Herb, sew long straight stitches (see page 126) for the daisy stems.

Using a yarn needle and Cedar Green, sew long straight stitches for the yellow flower stems. Work short straight stitches either side of the stems for leaves.

Using a yarn needle and Camel, sew long straight stitches for the lavender stems and work a few French knots in Bordeaux around the top of the stem for flowers.

To finish the bees, using a sewing needle and black sewing thread, stitch a few stripes around the body and work a French knot in the same thread for the eye. Sew the bees to the square. Using a yarn needle and White, sew a couple of small loops at the top of each bee's body for wings.

summer meadow

This autumn wreath gives just the smallest of nods to all the beautiful jewel-like colours that will appear throughout autumn, from the deep red of the toadstools, to the rich terracotta leaves to the burst of warmth in the Michaelmas daisies. Quick and simple to make, this is a perfect stash-buster project.

autumn wreath

SKILL RATING ● ● ●

YARN AND MATERIALS

FOR THE BACKGROUND SQUARE:
Rowan Handknit Cotton (100% cotton), DK (light worsted) weight, 85m (92yd) per 50g (1¾oz) ball
  1 ball of Linen shade 205 (off-white) (A)
  Small amount of Warm shade 379 (peach) (B)

FOR THE FLOWERS AND LEAVES:
Cascade Heritage (75% wool, 25% nylon), 4-ply (fingering) weight, 400m (437yd) per 100g (3½oz) skein (hank)
  Small amounts of:
  Cinnamon shade 5640 (reddish brown)
  Cedar Green shade 5684 (dark green)
  Tutu shade 5613 (pink)
  Wine shade 5663 (red)
  White shade 5682

Wired paper cord/thick string

HOOK AND EQUIPMENT

3mm (US D) crochet hook
2.5mm (US B-1 to C-2) crochet hook
Yarn needle
Blocking pins and mat
Hot glue gun

TENSION (GAUGE)
Exact tension is not important for this project.

FINISHED MEASUREMENTS
11.5 x 11.5cm (4½ x 4½in)

ABBREVIATIONS
See page 127.

BACKGROUND SQUARE
Using a 3mm (US D) hook and A, ch23.
Row 1: Starting in second ch from hook, 1dc in back bump of each ch to end, turn. (*22 sts*)
Row 2: Ch1 (does not count as st), 1dc in each st, turn.
Rows 3-22: Rep Row 2.
Fasten off.

Edging
Round 1: Using a 2.5mm (US B-1 to C-2) hook and A, with RS facing join in yarn at centre bottom of square with a sl st, 1dc in same st, *1dc in each st to corner, 3dc in corner st, 1dc in each row-end to next corner, 3dc in corner st; rep from * once more, 1dc in each st to beg of round, sl st to join. Fasten off and sew in ends (see page 123).
Round 2: With RS facing, join B at centre bottom with a sl stBLO, *3dcBLO in next st, sl stBLO in each of next 2 sts; rep from * to beg of round, sl st to join.
Fasten off and sew in ends.

WREATH BASE
Take a long length of wired paper cord or thick string and wind several circles on top of each other to get the required thickness for your wreath base, approx. 1cm (⅜in). Have a second length of wired paper cord/string ready to wind around the circles to secure in place as one thick circle.

LEAVES

(make 11 in Cinnamon, 11 in Cedar Green)
Using a 2.5mm (US B-1 to C-2) hook and either Cinnamon or Cedar Green, ch7.
Round 1: Starting in second ch from hook, sl st in each of next 2 ch, 1dc in each of next 2 ch, 2dc in each of last 2 ch, ch1 across bottom, working down opposite side of chain, sl st in next ch, 1dc in each of next 3 ch, sl st in each of next 2 ch.
Fasten off.

MICHAELMAS DAISIES

(make 5)
Using a 2.5mm (US B-1 to C-2) hook and Tutu, make a magic ring.
Round 1: *Ch3, starting in second ch from hook, sl st in each of next 2 ch back to magic ring, sl st in ring; rep from * 4 times making 5 petals in total.
Pull up magic ring.
Fasten off and sew in ends.

TOADSTOOLS

(make 7)
Using a 2.5mm (US B-1 to C-2) hook and Wine, make a magic ring.
Round 1: 6dc into ring. (*6 sts*)
Round 2: [2dc in next st, 1dc in each of next 2 sts] twice. (*8 sts*)
Round 3: 2dc in next st, 1dc in each of next 7 sts, sl st to join. (*9 sts*)
Fasten off.

FINISHING

Block the square (see page 123).
　Use a hot glue gun to stick the wreath base in the centre of the square.
　Start by sticking two thirds of the leaves onto the base.
　Using a yarn needle and Cinnamon, work a French knot (see page 127) in the centre of each daisy, then add the daisies to the wreath.
　Use a yarn needle and White to work small dots onto the top of each toadstool, then stick the toadstools to the wreath.
　Add the remaining leaves between the daisies and toadstools.

With his toadstool umbrella keeping him sheltered from autumn rain and falling leaves, this little hedgehog is hurrying home to warm up. Whether made as a picture square to be framed or added in with other autumn squares to make bunting, this creates all the autumn cosiness needed as we head into the darker months. For the hedgehog prickles I used a fur yarn, but any eyelash yarn or fluffy textured yarn would work equally well.

autumn hedgehog with toadstool umbrella

SKILL RATING ● ● ●

YARN AND MATERIALS

FOR THE BACKGROUND SQUARE:
Rowan Handknit Cotton (100% cotton), DK (light worsted) weight, 85m (92yd) per 50g (1¾oz) ball
  1 ball of Linen shade 205 (off-white) (A)
  Small amount of Warm shade 379 (peach) (B)

FOR THE HEDGEHOG, TOADSTOOL AND FLOWERS:
King Cole Luxury Fur (90% nylon, 10% polyester), fur/eyelash yarn, 92m (100yd) per 100g (3½oz) ball
  Small amount of Impala shade 4204 (light grey)

Cascade Heritage (75% wool, 25% nylon), 4-ply (fingering) weight, 400m (437yd) per 100g (3½oz) skein (hank)
  Small amounts of:
  Cinnamon shade 5640 (reddish brown)
  Red shade 5607
  White shade 5682
  Tutu shade 5613 (pink)
  Sage shade 5635 (soft green)

1 small safety eye

Black yarn

HOOK AND EQUIPMENT

3mm (US D) crochet hook

2.5mm (US B-1 to C-2) crochet hook

Stitch marker

Yarn needle

Blocking pins and mat

Sewing needle and thread

TENSION (GAUGE)
Exact tension is not important for this project.

FINISHED MEASUREMENTS
11.5 x 11.5cm (4½ x 4½in)

ABBREVIATIONS
See page 127.

BACKGROUND SQUARE

Using a 3mm (US D) hook and A, ch23.
Row 1: Starting in second ch from hook, 1dc in back bump of each ch to end, turn. (*22 sts*)
Row 2: Ch1 (does not count as st), 1dc in each st, turn.
Rows 3–22: Rep Row 2.
Fasten off.

Edging

Round 1: Using a 2.5mm (US B-1 to C-2) hook and A, with RS facing join in yarn at centre bottom of square with a sl st, 1dc in same st, *1dc in each st to corner, 3dc in corner st, 1dc in each row-end to next corner, 3dc in corner st; rep from * once more, 1dc in each st to beg of round, sl st to join.
Fasten off and sew in ends (see page 123).
Round 2: With RS facing, join B at centre bottom with a sl stBLO, *3dcBLO in next st, sl stBLO in each of next 2 sts; rep from * to beg of round, sl st to join.
Fasten off and sew in ends.

HEDGEHOG

Using a 2.5mm (US B-1 to C-2) hook and Cinnamon, make a magic ring.
Round 1: 8dc into ring. (*8 sts*)
Round 2: [1dc in next st, 2dc in next st] 4 times. (*12 sts*)
Round 3: [1dc in each of next 2 sts, 2dc in next st] 4 times. (*16 sts*)
Round 4: 2dc in next st, 1dc in each of next 6 sts, 2dc in each of next 2 sts, 1dc in each of next 6 sts, 2dc in next st. (*20 sts*)
Rounds 5 and 6: 1dc in each st.
Round 7: [1dc in each of next 9 sts, 2dc in next st] twice. (*22 sts*)
Round 8: 1dc in each st.
Round 9: [1dc in each of next 6 sts, 2dc in next st] 3 times, 1dc in next st. (*25 sts*)
Rounds 10–13: 1dc in each st.
Round 14: [1dc in each of next 6 sts, dc2tog] 3 times, 1dc in next st. (*22 sts*)

Round 15: [1dc in each of next 9 sts, dc2tog] twice. (*20 sts*)
Round 16: [1dc in each of next 3 sts, dc2tog] 4 times. (*16 sts*)
Round 17: 1dc in each of next 6 sts, [dc2tog] twice, 1dc in each of next 6 sts. (*14 sts*)
Round 18: 2dc in next st, 1dc in each of next 12 sts, 2dc in next st. (*16 sts*)
Round 19: 1dc in each st.
Round 20: 2dc in next st, 1dc in each of next 6 sts, 2dc in each of next 2 sts, 1dc in each of next 7 sts. (*19 sts*)
Round 21: 1dc in each of next 9 sts, 2tr in next st, 1dc in each of next 9 sts (hedgehog nose). (*20 sts*)
Round 22: 1dc in each st.
Round 23: 1dc in each of next 7 sts, miss next 6 sts (missed sts will flatten to form top of nose), 1dc in each of next 7 sts, PM.
You now have a new round of 14 sts.
Round 24: 1dc in each of next 7 sts, 2dc in next st, 1dc in each st to marker. (*15 sts*)
Round 25: 1dc in next st, dc2tog, 1dc in each of next 4 sts, [dc2tog] twice, 1dc in each st to marker. (*12 sts*)
Round 26: [Dc2tog] 6 times. (*6 sts*)
Fasten off and close opening.

ARMS
(make 2)
Using a 2.5mm (US B-1 to C-2) hook and Cinnamon, ch8.
Row 1: Starting in second ch from hook, (1htr, 1dc) in next ch, sl st in back bump of each ch to end.
Fasten off.

FEET
(make 2)
Using a 2.5mm (US B-1 to C-2) hook and Cinnamon, ch8.
Row 1: Starting in second ch from hook, (1dc, 1htr) in next ch, sl st in back bump of each ch to end.
Fasten off.

TOADSTOOL
Using a 2.5mm (US B-1 to C-2) hook and Red, make a magic ring.
Round 1: 12dc into ring. (*12 sts*)
Round 2: 2dc in each st. (*24 sts*)
Round 3: 1dc in each st.
Round 4: [1dc in next st, 2dc in next st] 12 times. (*36 sts*)
Rounds 5 and 6: 1dc in each st.
Round 7: [1dc in each of next 2 sts, 2dc in next st] 12 times. (*48 sts*)
Rounds 8–10: 1dc in each st.
Round 11: 2dc in next st, 1dc in each of next 22 sts, 2dc in each of next 2 sts, 1dc in each of next 22 sts, 2dc in next st. (*52 sts*)
Round 12: 2dc in next st, 1dc in each of next 24 sts, 2dc in each of next 2 sts, 1dc in each of next 24 sts, 2dc in next st. (*56 sts*)
Round 13: 1dc in each st.
Fasten off Red.
Round 14: Join White, 1dcBLO in each st.
Fasten off.

STALK
Using a 2.5mm (US B-1 to C-2) hook and White, ch21.
Row 1: Starting in second ch from hook, 1dc in each ch to end, turn. (*20 sts*)
Rows 2–4: Ch1 (does not count as st), 1dc in each st, turn.
Fasten off leaving a yarn tail for sewing.

MICHAELMAS DAISIES (MAKE 2)
Using a 2.5mm (US B-1 to C-2) hook and Tutu, make a magic ring.
Round 1: *Ch3, starting in second ch from hook, sl st in each of next 2 ch back to magic ring, sl st in ring; rep from * four more times to make 5 petals in total.
Pull up the magic ring.
Fasten off and sew in ends.

FINISHING
Block the square (see page 123).

Using a yarn needle and the fur/eyelash yarn, starting at the centre top of the hedgehog head, oversew the yarn from the edge to halfway across the head and body to create the prickled back. Insert the safety eye or work a French knot (see page 127) in black yarn.

Using a sewing needle and thread, stitch the hedgehog to the square, attaching the arms and feet at the same time. Use a small amount of black yarn to sew on a nose.

Using a yarn needle and White, work French knots on the toadstool top. Use the yarn tail to sew the long edges of the stalk together. Position the stalk so that the hedgehog is holding it, then place the end inside the toadstool top and stitch all in place.

Using a yarn needle and Cinnamon, work a French knot in the centre of each Michaelmas daisy. Sew the daisies in place and work a couple of straight stitches (see page 126) in Sage from the flowers to the hedgehog's hand as stalks.

Work straight stitches in Sage for the grass along the bottom edge of the square. Sew pairs of small straight stitches in Cinnamon to create falling leaves in the background.

When the mistletoe comes out the festive season has arrived! This little sprig has the tiniest of white bells for berries and is worked to create a 3-D effect so that the bunch stands out from the square. Each leaf and stem is worked individually, in the round, and then the stems are stitched together to finish.

winter mistletoe sprig

SKILL RATING ● ○ ○

YARN AND MATERIALS

FOR THE BACKGROUND SQUARE:
Rowan Summerlite 4 ply (100% cotton), 4-ply (fingering) weight, 175m (191yd) per 50g (1¾oz) ball
  1 ball of Aqua shade 433 (turquoise) (A)

Cascade Ultra Pima (100% cotton), DK (light worsted) weight, 200m (220yd) per 100g (3½oz) skein (hank)
  Small amount of Tomato shade 3823 (red) (B)

FOR THE MISTLETOE:
Rowan Summerlite 4 ply (100% cotton), 4-ply (fingering) weight, 175m (191yd) per 50g (1¾oz) ball
  Small amount of Mint shade 451 (light green)

4 small white craft bells

Small amount of red ribbon

Glitter glue (optional)

HOOK AND EQUIPMENT
3mm (US D) crochet hook

2.5mm (US B-1 to C-2) crochet hook

Yarn needle

Blocking pins and mat

Sewing needle and thread

TENSION (GAUGE)
Exact tension is not important for this project.

FINISHED MEASUREMENTS
10 x 10cm (4 x 4in)

ABBREVIATIONS
See page 127.

BACKGROUND SQUARE
Using a 3mm (US D) hook and A, ch23.
Row 1: Starting in second ch from hook, 1dc in back bump of each ch to end, turn. (*22 sts*)
Row 2: Ch1 (does not count as st), 1dc in each st, turn.
Rows 3–22: Rep Row 2.
Fasten off.

EDGING
Round 1: Using a 2.5mm (US B-1 to C-2) hook and A, with RS facing join in yarn at centre bottom of square with a sl st, 1dc in same st, *1dc in each st to corner, 3dc in corner st, 1dc in each row-end to next corner, 3dc in corner st; rep from * once more, 1dc in each st to beg of round, sl st to join. Fasten off and sew in ends (see page 123).
Round 2: With RS facing, join B at centre bottom with a sl stBLO, *sl stBLO in each of next 2 sts, ch3; rep from * to beg of round, sl st to join.
Fasten off and sew in ends.

LARGE MISTLETOE LEAF
(make 3)
Using a 2.5mm (US B-1 to C-2) hook and Mint, make a magic ring.
Round 1: 4dc into ring. (*4 sts*)
Round 2: [1dc in next st, 2dc in next st] twice. (*6 sts*)
Round 3: 1dc in next st, 2dc in next st, 1 dc in each of next 3 sts, 2dc in next st. (*8 sts*)

winter mistletoe sprig

Rounds 4–6: 1dc in each st.
Round 7: Dc2tog, 1dc in each of next 6 sts. (*7 sts*)
Round 8: Dc2tog, 1dc in each of next 5 sts. (*6 sts*)
Round 9: 1dc in each st.
Round 10: Dc2tog, 1dc in each of next 4 sts. (*5 sts*)
Round 11: 1dc in each st.
Round 12: [Dc2tog] twice, 1dc in next st, sl st to join. (*3 sts*)
Do not fasten off.

Stem
Row 1: Ch13, starting in second ch from hook, 1dc in each ch to end.
Fasten off.

SMALL MISTLETOE LEAF
(make 3)
Using a 2.5mm (US B-1 to C-2) hook and Mint, make a magic ring.
Round 1: 4dc into ring. (*4 sts*)
Round 2: 2dc in next st, 1dc in each of next 3 sts. (*5 sts*)
Rounds 3–6: 1dc in each st.
Round 7: Dc2tog, 1dc in each of next 3 sts. (*4 sts*)
Round 8: [Dc2tog] twice. (*2 sts*)
Round 9: 1dc in each of next 2 sts, sl st to join.
Do not fasten off.

Stem
Row 1: Ch17, starting in second ch from hook, 1dc in each ch to end.
Fasten off.

FINISHING
Block the square (see page 123).
   Stitch the stems of one large and one small leaf together, with the curves of the leaves facing inwards.
   Position the three mistletoe sprigs on the square so that they make a bunch, with all the stems together/on top of each other. Using a sewing needle and thread, stitch the one main stem to the square. If needed, stitch a couple of holding stitches at the base of the leaves to hold in position but keep the 3-D effect by not stitching all the way around.
   Using a sewing needle and thread, sew the bells onto the mistletoe for berries.
   Thread the ribbon into a yarn needle and thread each end from the back of the square to the front and then tie in a bow. If needed, anchor the ends of the bow with a couple of holding stitches.
   Paint some glitter glue onto the edges of the leaves to catch the light (optional).

Even penguins sometimes need to wrap up warm and this little one has his matching hat and scarf all ready for those snowy days. This square would be perfect for adding to some winter bunting or displayed in a box frame as a picture.

winter penguin

SKILL RATING ● ● ○

YARN AND MATERIALS

FOR THE BACKGROUND SQUARE:
Rowan Summerlite 4 ply (100% cotton), 4-ply (fingering) weight, 175m (191yd) per 50g (1¾oz) ball
  1 ball of Aqua shade 433 (turquoise) (A)

Cascade Ultra Pima (100% cotton), DK (light worsted) weight, 200m (220yd) per 100g (3½oz) skein (hank)
  Small amount of Tomato shade 3823 (red) (B)

FOR THE PENGUIN, HAT AND SCARF:
Cascade Heritage (75% wool, 25% nylon), 4-ply (fingering) weight, 400m (437yd) per 100g (3½oz) skein (hank)
  Small amounts of:
  Limestone shade 5681 (light grey)
  Forged Iron shade 5736 (dark grey)
  White shade 5682
  Mustard shade 5652 (yellow)
  Herb shade 5658 (green)
  Red shade 5607

Pair of small back safety eyes

HOOK AND EQUIPMENT
3mm (US D) crochet hook
2.5mm (US B-1 to C-2) crochet hook
2mm (US steel size 4) crochet hook
Yarn needle
Blocking pins and mat
Sewing needle and thread

TENSION (GAUGE)
Exact tension is not important for this project.

FINISHED MEASUREMENTS
10 x 10cm (4 x 4in)

ABBREVIATIONS
See page 127.

BACKGROUND SQUARE

Using a 3mm (US D) hook and A, ch23.
Row 1: Starting in second ch from hook, 1dc in back bump of each ch to end, turn. (*22 sts*)
Row 2: Ch1 (does not count as st), 1dc in each st, turn.
Rows 3–22: Rep Row 2.
Fasten off.

Edging
Round 1: Using a 2.5mm (US B-1 to C-2) hook and A, with RS facing join in yarn at centre bottom of square with a sl st, 1dc in same st, *1dc in each st to corner, 3dc in corner st, 1dc in each row-end to next corner, 3dc in corner st; rep from * once more, 1dc in each st to beg of round, sl st to join. Fasten off and sew in ends (see page 123).
Round 2: With RS facing, join B at centre bottom with a sl st BLO, *sl stBLO in each of next 2 sts, ch3; rep from * to beg of round, sl st to join.
Fasten off and sew in ends.

PENGUIN BODY

Using a 2.5mm (US B-1 to C-2) hook and Limestone, make a magic ring.
Round 1: 6dc into ring. (*6 sts*)
Round 2: [2dc in next st] 6 times. (*12 sts*)
Round 3: [1dc in next st, 2dc in next st] 6 times. (*18 sts*)
Round 4: [1dc in each of next 2 sts, 2dc in next st] 6 times. (*24 sts*)
Round 5: [1dc in each of next 3 sts, 2dc in next st] 6 times. (*30 sts*)
Rounds 6–10: 1dc in each st.
Round 11: Dc2tog, 1dc in each of next 13 sts, dc2tog, 1dc in each of next 13 sts. (*28 sts*)
Round 12: Dc2tog, 1dc in each of next 12 sts, dc2tog, 1dc in each of next 12 sts. (*26 sts*)

Round 13: Dc2tog, 1dc in each of next 11 sts, dc2tog, 1dc in each of next 11 sts. (*24 sts*)
Round 14: 1dc in each st.
Fasten off Limestone, join in Forged Iron.
Rounds 15–17: 1dc in each st.
Round 18: Dc2tog, 1dc in each of next 10 sts, dc2tog, 1dc in each of next 10 sts. (*22 sts*)
Rounds 19–22: 1dc in each st.
Round 23: Dc2tog, 1dc in each of next 9 sts, dc2tog, 1dc in each of next 9 sts. (*20 sts*)
Round 24: [Dc2tog] 10 times. (*10 sts*)
Fasten off and sew up top.

WINGS
(make 2)
Using a 2.5mm (US B-1 to C-2) hook and Forged Iron, make a magic ring.
Round 1: 4dc into ring. (*4 sts*)
Round 2: [1dc in next st, 2dc in next st] twice. (*6 sts*)
Rounds 3–9: 1dc in each st.
Fasten off.

FEET
(make 2)
Using a 2.5mm (US B-1 to C-2) hook and Forged Iron, ch5.
Round 1: Starting in second ch from hook, 1dc in each ch to last ch, 2dc in last ch, 1dc in each ch down opposite side of chain, 1dc in row-end. (*9 sts*)
Rounds 2 and 3: 1dc in each st.
At end of Round 3, sl st to join.
Fasten off.

EYES
(make 1)
Using a 2.5mm (US B-1 to C-2) hook and White, ch10.
Row 1: Starting in second ch from hook, 1dc in each ch to end, turn. (*9 sts*)
Round 2: Ch1 (does not count as st), 1dc in next st, 1tr in next st, 1dtr in next st, ch1, sl st in each of next 3 sts, ch1, 1dtr in next st, 1tr in next st, 1dc in next st, do not turn, 1dc in each row-end down left-hand side, 1dc in each st along bottom edge, 1dc in each row-end up right-hand side, sl st to join.
Fasten off.

BEAK
Using 2mm (US steel size 4) hook and Mustard, ch4.
Row 1: Starting in second ch from hook, 1dc in each ch to end, turn. (*3 sts*)
Row 2: Ch1 (does not count as st), dc2tog, 1dc in next st, turn. (*2 sts*)
Row 3: Dc2tog.
Fasten off.

HAT
Using a 2.5mm (US B-1 to C-2) hook and Herb, make a magic ring.
Round 1: 8dc into ring. (*8 sts*)
Round 2: Join in Red, leaving Herb at back, using Red [2dc in next st] 8 times. (*16 sts*)
Round 3: Bring up Herb, leaving Red at back, using Herb [1dc in next st, 2dc in next st] 8 times. (*24 sts*)
Round 4: Bring up Red, leaving Herb at back, using Red [1dc in each of next 2 sts, 2dc in next st] 8 times. (*32 sts*)
Round 5: Bring up Herb, leaving Red at back, using Herb 1dc in each st.
Fasten off Herb, cont in Red only.
Round 6: [1dc in each of next 14 sts, dc2tog] twice. (*30 sts*)
Rounds 7 and 8: 1dc in each st.
At end of Round 8, sl st to join.
Fasten off.

SCARF
Using a 2.5mm (US B-1 to C-2) hook and Red, ch46.
Row 1: Starting in second ch from hook, 1dc in each ch to end. (*45 sts*)
Fasten off.

FINISHING
Block the square (see page 123).
   Insert the two safety eyes into the centre of each 'eye arch' on the eyes piece. Sew the eyes piece onto the penguin.
   Fold the beak triangle down the centre from top edge to point to make a small beak shape. Use the yarn tails to secure.
   Using a yarn needle and a doubled strand of Red work a large French knot (see page 127) at the top of the hat. To make the bobble bigger if required, oversew over the top of the French knot several times then fasten off.
   Place the hat and scarf on the penguin and use a couple of stitches to secure.
   Stitch the beak in to place just below and between the eyes. Stitch the wings and feet onto the penguin using a sewing needle and thread.
   Stitch the completed penguin onto the square.
   Using White in a yarn needle, work French knots over the background and along the bottom of the square for snow.

chapter 2
greetings squares

Everyone loves a happy ever after and this little square says it perfectly as the wedding car drives off into the distance! Perfect for personalising with initials and your chosen colours, this is a very simple but beautifully unique gift.

wedding car

SKILL RATING ● ○ ○

YARN AND MATERIALS

FOR THE BACKGROUND SQUARE:
Rowan Summerlite 4 ply (100% cotton), 4-ply (fingering) weight, 175m (191yd) per 50g (1¾oz) ball
- 1 ball of Ecru shade 436 (off-white) (A)

Cascade Ultra Pima (100% cotton), DK (light worsted) weight, 200m (220yd) per 100g (3½oz) skein (hank)
- Small amount of Shell shade 3854 (light pink) (B)

FOR THE CAR
Cascade Heritage (75% wool, 25% nylon), 4-ply (fingering) weight, 400m (437yd) per 100g (3½oz) skein (hank)
- Small amounts of:
- White shade 5682
- Camel shade 5610 (beige)
- Forged Iron shade 5736 (dark grey)
- Lemon shade 5644 (light yellow)
- Golden Yellow shade 5752 (dark yellow)
- Herb shade 5658 (green)
- Sage shade 5635 (soft green)

Anchor Artiste Metallic (20% polyester, 80% viscose), 4-ply (fingering) weight, 100m (109yd) per 25g (⅞oz) ball
- Small amount of Gold shade 300

Small piece of spare cardboard

HOOK AND EQUIPMENT
3mm (US D) crochet hook

2.5mm (US B-1 to C-2) crochet hook

2mm (US steel size 4) crochet hook

Yarn needle

Blocking pins and mat

Pencil

Scissors or craft knife to cut card

Sewing needle and thread

TENSION (GAUGE)
Exact tension is not important for this project.

FINISHED MEASUREMENTS
10 x 10cm (4 x 4in)

ABBREVIATIONS
See page 127.

BACKGROUND SQUARE
Using a 3mm (US D) hook and A, ch23.
Row 1: Starting in second ch from hook, 1dc in back bump of each ch to end, turn. (*22 sts*)
Row 2: Ch1 (does not count as st), 1dc in each st, turn.
Rows 3–22: Rep Row 2.
Fasten off.

Edging
Round 1: Using a 2.5mm (US B-1 to C-2) hook and A, with RS facing join in yarn at centre bottom of square with a sl st, 1dc in same st, *1dc in each st to corner, 3dc in corner st, 1dc in each row-end to next corner, 3dc in corner st; rep from * once more, 1dc in each st to beg of round, sl st to join.
Fasten off and sew in ends (see page 123).
Round 2: With RS facing, join B at centre bottom with a sl stBLO, *1dcBLO in each of next 2 sts, ch2; rep from * to beg of round, sl st to join.
Fasten off and sew in ends.

WEDDING CAR
Using a 2.5mm (US B-1 to C-2) hook and 2 strands of White held together, ch17.
Row 1: Starting in second ch from hook, 1dc in back bump of each ch to end, turn. (*16 sts*)
Rows 2–6: Ch1 (does not count as st throughout), 1dc in each st, turn.
Row 7: Ch1, dc2tog, 1dc in each of next 12 sts, dc2tog, turn. (*14 sts*)
Row 8: Ch1, sl st in next st, 1dc in each of next 12 sts, sl st in next st, turn.
Row 9: Ch1, skip sl st, 1dc in each of next 12 sts, turn. (*12 sts*)
Rows 10–12: Ch1, 1dc in each st to end, turn.
Row 13: Ch1, dc2tog, 1dc in next st, 1htr in each of next 6 sts, 1dc in next st, dc2tog. (*10 sts*)
Fasten off.

Edging
Round 1: Join 2 strands of White at bottom right-hand corner, work dc evenly all around edge of car, working sl st at wheel hub shaping.
Fasten off.
Round 2: Using 2mm (US steel size 4) hook, join Camel at bottom right-hand corner, 1dc in each st around edge of car, working sl st at wheel hub shaping, to create a bit of a curve that will increase 3-D effect.

Round 4: [1dc in each of next 2 sts, 2dc in next st] 6 times. (24 sts)
Rounds 5 and 6: 1dc in each st.
Round 7: Dc2tog, 1dc in each of next 10 sts, dc2tog, 1dc in each of next 10 sts. (22 sts)
Round 8: Dc2tog, 1dc in each of next 9 sts, dc2tog, 1dc in each of next 9 sts. (20 sts)
Round 9: [1dc in each of next 3 sts, dc2tog] 4 times. (16 sts)
Round 10: [1 dc in each of next 2 sts, dc2tog] 4 times. (12 sts)
Round 11: [Dc2tog] 6 times. (6 sts)
Round 12: Dc2tog, 1dc in each of next 2 sts, dc2tog. (4 sts)
Round 13: 1dc in each st, sl st to join.
Fasten off.

FINISHING

Block the square (see page 123).

Draw around the outline of the car onto a small piece of card. Add a border of about 1cm (³⁄₈in) all around the outline and cut out.

Using Camel work sl st surface crochet (see page 126) to add detail to the rear and boot of the car, using the photo as a guide.

Thread a length of Gold into a yarn needle and stitch a window shape onto the car in long, horizontal satin stitch (see page 127). Also using Gold, stitch rear lights and a handle for the car boot.

Using a sewing needle and thread stitch the bumper to the car and then, using Forged Iron, stitch a couple of long oversew stitches so that the bumper looks attached to the car. Also using Forged Iron, stitch a small number plate.

Using the greens and yellows work a small floral garland across the back of the car using running stitches and French Knots (see pages 126 and 127).

Stitch the car to the square around the side edges and the top, leaving the bottom edge open.

On the cardboard cut-out fold the 1cm (³⁄₈in) border under, snipping where needed around the curves. Insert this into the bottom edge of the car to give it a solid shape. Trim the cardboard as needed to ensure a snug fit.

Stitch the wheels to the square, inserting the top of each wheel just under the back edge of the car.

Stitch initials to the balloons if desired and then stitch onto the square, using the contrasting yellow to make the ribbon and string. Stitch a small heart between the two balloons using short running stitches.

BUMPER

Using 2mm (US steel size 4) hook and Forged Iron, ch25.
Round 1: Starting in second ch from hook, sl st in each ch to last ch, (sl st, 2dc) in last ch, sl st in each ch along opposite side of chain to last ch, (sl st, 2dc) in last ch.
Round 2: 1dc in each st to corner, 2dc in corner st, 1dc in each st to last st, 2dc in last st, sl st to join.
Fasten off.

WHEELS

(make 2)
Using 2mm (US steel size 4) hook and Forged Iron, make a magic ring.
Round 1: 6dc into ring. (6 sts)
Rounds 2–5: 1dc in each st.
Round 6: 1dc in each st, sl st to join.
Fasten off.

BALLOONS

(make 1 in Lemon, 1 in Golden Yellow)
Using a 2.5mm (US B-1 to C-2) hook, make a magic ring.
Round 1: 6dc into ring. (6 sts)
Round 2: [2dc in next st] 6 times. (12 sts)
Round 3: [1dc in next st, 2dc in next st] 6 times. (18 sts)

This little square is such a fun make and would work perfectly as a unique handmade wedding card or gift, especially if the colours are matched to co-ordinate with the wedding colours. The cake is made to stand out from the square and the decorations are sewn on separately with very simple stitches and French knots.

wedding cake

SKILL RATING ● ● ○

YARN AND MATERIALS

FOR THE BACKGROUND SQUARE:
Rowan Summerlite 4 ply (100% cotton), 4-ply (fingering) weight, 175m (191yd) per 50g (1¾oz) ball
- 1 ball of Ecru shade 436 (off-white) (A)

Cascade Ultra Pima (100% cotton), DK (light worsted) weight, 200m (220yd) per 100g (3½oz) skein (hank)
- Small amount of Shell shade 3854 (light pink) (B)

FOR THE CAKE:
Cascade Heritage (75% wool, 25% nylon), 4-ply (fingering) weight, 400m (437yd) per 100g (3½oz) skein (hank)
- Small amounts of:
  White shade 5682
  Herb shade 5658 (green)
  Sage shade 5635 (soft green)
  Lemon shade 5644 (light yellow)
  Golden Yellow shade 5752 (dark yellow)

Anchor Artiste Metallic (20% polyester, 80% viscose), 4-ply (fingering) weight, 100m (109yd) per 25g (⅞oz) ball
- Small amount of Gold shade 300

Small amount of toy filling

HOOK AND EQUIPMENT
3mm (US D) crochet hook
2.5mm (US B-1 to C-2) crochet hook
Yarn needle
Blocking pins and mat
Sewing needle and thread

TENSION (GAUGE)
Exact tension is not important for this project.

FINISHED MEASUREMENTS
10 x 10cm (4 x 4in)

ABBREVIATIONS
See page 127.

BACKGROUND SQUARE

Using a 3mm (US D) hook and A, ch23.
Row 1: Starting in second ch from hook, 1dc in back bump of each ch to end, turn. (*22 sts*)
Row 2: Ch1 (does not count as st), 1dc in each st, turn.
Rows 3–22: Rep Row 2.
Fasten off.

Edging
Round 1: Using a 2.5mm (US B-1 to C-2) hook and A, with RS facing join in yarn at centre bottom of square with a sl st, 1dc in same st, *1dc in each st to corner, 3dc in corner st, 1dc in each row-end to next corner, 3dc in corner st; rep from * once more, 1dc in each st to beg of round, sl st to join.
Fasten off and sew in ends (see page 123).
Round 2: With RS facing, join B at centre bottom with a sl stBLO, *1dcBLO in each of next 2 sts, ch2; rep from * to beg of round, sl st to join.
Fasten off and sew in ends.

WEDDING CAKE BOTTOM LAYER

Using a 2.5mm (US B-1 to C-2) hook and White, ch16.
Row 1: Starting in second ch from hook, 1dc in each ch to end, turn. (*15 sts*)
Row 2: Ch1 (does not count as st throughout), dc2tog, 1dc in each of next 11 sts, dc2tog, turn. (*13 sts*)
Row 3: Ch1, dc2tog, 1dc in each of next 9 sts, dc2tog, turn. (*11 sts*)
Row 4: Ch1, dc2tog, 1dc in each of next 3 sts, 1htr in next st, 1dc in each of next 3 sts, dc2tog. (*9 sts*)
Fasten off.

Bottom edging
Join 2 strands of White at right-hand side of curved edge, work 18dc evenly around curved edge of base. (*18 sts*)
Fasten off.

Sides
Row 1: Join 1 strand of White at right-hand side of curved edge of base, 1dcBLO in each st, turn. (*18 sts*)
Rows 2–8: Ch1, 1dc in each st, turn.
Fasten off.

Side edging
Join 2 strands of White in unworked front loop at end of Row 1, work crab stitch from left to right working in FLO.
Fasten off.

Top
Row 1: Working in BLO of Row 8, join 1 strand of White at right-hand side, [4dcBLO, dc2togBLO] 3 times, turn. (*15 sts*)
Row 2: Ch1, [dc2tog] 7 times, 1dc in last st, turn. (*8 sts*)
Row 3: Ch1, 1dc in each st.
Fasten off.

Top edging
Join 2 strands of White in unworked front loop at end of Row 1, work crab stitch from left to right working in FLO.
Fasten off.

WEDDING CAKE TOP LAYER
Using a 2.5mm (US B-1 to C-2) hook and White, ch8.
Row 1: Starting in second ch from hook, 1dc in each ch to end, turn. (*7 sts*)
Row 2: Ch1, dc2tog, 1dc in each of next 3 dc, dc2tog, turn. (*5 sts*)
Row 3: Ch1, dc2tog, 1htr in next st, dc2tog. (*3 sts*)
Fasten off.

Top edging
Join 2 strands of White at right-hand side of curved edge, 1dc in each st and row-end around curved edge. (*9 sts*)
Fasten off.

Sides
Row 1: Join 1 strand of White at right-hand side of curved edge, 1dcBLO in each st, turn. (*9 sts*)
Rows 2–8: Ch1, 1dc in each st, turn. (*9 sts*)
Fasten off.
To neaten top cake edges, work dc up each side edge.

Side edging
Join 2 strands of White in unworked front loop at end of Row 1, work crab stitch from left to right working in FLO.
Fasten off.

FINISHING
Block the square (see page 123).

Stitch the bottom layer of the cake to the bottom edge of the square, making sure that you are keeping the 3-D effect. Stuff the cake through the open semi-circle at the top.

Place the smaller cake on top of the one attached to the square; the 'base' will be the top of the cake. Stitch one of the side edges of the top cake to the square, again keeping the curved 3-D shape. Stuff the top cake and then stitch on the other side edge. If needed add any top ups of stuffing in the small opening at the base of the top cake. Stitch along the bottom edge of the top cake to join it to the top of the bottom cake.

Using Gold in a yarn needle, oversew along each of the three crab-stitch edges. Use one of the greens to stitch a 'garland' of running stitches (see page 126) all around the cake. Use the second green to stitch leaves, by working two running stitches side by side.

Use both Lemon and Golden Yellow to stitch French knots (see page 127) all along the garland.

Decorate the top of the cake by using double-stranded yarn to make bigger French knots for roses, worked on top of each other to create a raised posy effect. Use one of the greens to add a few leaves to the top of the roses.

wedding cake

valentine's bouquet

With a bunch of red roses being the quintessential symbol of love, this tiny bouquet makes for the perfect Valentine greeting when mounted onto some card. It is so quick and simple to make but gives maximum impact. And while perfect for 14th February, this square can also be used at any other time of the year for a birthday, new home or get well soon message.

SKILL RATING ● ○ ○

YARN AND MATERIALS

FOR THE BACKGROUND SQUARE:
Rowan Summerlite 4 ply (100% cotton), 4-ply (fingering) weight, 175m (191yd) per 50g (1¾oz) ball
- 1 ball of Seashell shade 437 (white) (A)

Cascade Ultra Pima (100% cotton), DK (light worsted) weight, 200m (220yd) per 100g (3½oz) skein (hank)
- Small amount of Light Grey shade 3808 (B)

FOR THE ROSES:
Cascade Heritage (75% wool, 25% nylon), 4-ply (fingering) weight, 400m (437yd) per 100g (3½oz) skein (hank)
- Small amounts of:
- Red shade 5607
- Wine shade 5663 (dark red)
- Sage shade 5635 (soft green)

9 stems of 26-gauge florist's wire in dark green

Short length of ribbon

HOOK AND EQUIPMENT

3mm (US D) crochet hook

2.5mm (US B-1 to C-2) crochet hook

Yarn needle

Blocking pins and mat

Scissors to cut florist's wire

Sewing needle and thread

Hot glue gun

TENSION (GAUGE)
Exact tension is not important for this project.

FINISHED MEASUREMENTS
9.5 x 9.5cm (3¾ x 3¾in)

ABBREVIATIONS
See page 127.

40 greetings squares

BACKGROUND SQUARE

Using a 3mm (US D) hook and A, ch23.
Row 1: Starting in second ch from hook, 1dc in back bump of each ch to end, turn. (*22 sts*)
Row 2: Ch1 (does not count as st), 1dc in each st, turn.
Rows 3–22: Rep Row 2.
Fasten off.

Edging

Round 1: Using a 2.5mm (US B-1 to C-2) hook and A, with RS facing join in yarn at centre bottom of square with a sl st, 1dc in same st, *1dc in each st to corner, 3dc in corner st, 1dc in each row-end to next corner, 3dc in corner st; rep from * once more, 1dc in each st to beg of round, sl st to join.
Fasten off and sew in ends (see page 123).
Round 2: With RS facing, join B at centre bottom with a sl stBLO,* sl stBLO in each of next 2 sts, ch2; rep from * to beg of round, sl st to join.
Fasten off and sew in ends.

ROSES

(make 5 in Red, 4 in Wine)
Using a 2.5mm (US B-1 to C-2) hook, ch22.
Row 1: Starting in second ch from hook, sl st in each of next 2 ch, 1dc in each of next 2 ch, sl st in each of next 2 ch, 2htr in next ch, sl st in each of next 2 ch, 2htr in next ch, sl st in each of next 2 ch, 2htr in each of next 2 ch, sl st in each of next 2 ch, 2dtr in each of next 2 ch, sl st in each ch to end.
Fasten off, leaving a long yarn tail.

LEAF

(make 8)
Using a 2.5mm (US B-1 to C-2) hook, make a magic ring.
Row 1: Ch3, (1dtr, 1tr, sl st) into ring.
Close ring and fasten off.

FINISHING

Block the square (see page 123).

Use the yarn tail on each rose to run a gathering thread along the straight edge of the piece. Lightly pull up the thread and then, starting at the narrow end, roll up the strip to form the rose. Stitch to hold in place.

Cut the florist stems to the correct length. For each rose take one wire stem and bend over the tip of the wire to make a very small hook. Then thread the other end of the wire down through the top of a rose, pulling it down so that the hook catches on the inside of the rose. If needed, you could add a tiny drop of glue from a hot glue gun to the tip of the hook before pulling the stem down into the rose.

Once all the roses have stems, arrange them into a bouquet and wind a small piece of wire around to hold them all in place. Secure the bouquet to the square with some holding stitches and wrap a piece of ribbon around the wire to cover it, then tie to secure.

Stick or glue the rose heads in place and add the leaves in between the stems.

To give the ribbon tails some shape, twist them slightly and stitch in place.

Sometimes we all need a little love, whether for Valentine's day, a birthday, an anniversary or simply 'just because', and though tiny this square sends out the biggest hug and all the love possible. The heart couldn't be simpler to make and can be worked in any colour – a design that's perfect for using up your leftover yarn.

valentine's heart

SKILL RATING ● ○ ○

YARN AND MATERIALS
FOR THE BACKGROUND SQUARE:
Rowan Summerlite 4 ply (100% cotton), 4-ply (fingering) weight, 175m (191yd) per 50g (1¾oz) ball
  1 ball of Seashell shade 437 (white) (A)

Cascade Ultra Pima (100% cotton), DK (light worsted) weight, 200m (220yd) per 100g (3½oz) skein (hank)
  Small amount of Light Grey shade 3808 (B)

FOR THE HEART:
Cascade Heritage (75% wool, 25% nylon), 4-ply (fingering) weight, 400m (437yd) per 100g (3½oz) skein (hank)
  Small amount of Red shade 5607 (C)

Small amount of toy stuffing

HOOK AND EQUIPMENT
3mm (US D) crochet hook
2.5mm (US B-1 to C-2) crochet hook
Yarn needle
Blocking pins and mat
Sewing needle and thread

TENSION (GAUGE)
Exact tension is not important for this project.

MEASUREMENTS
9.5 x 9.5cm (3¾ x 3¾in)

ABBREVIATIONS
See page 127.

BACKGROUND SQUARE
Using a 3mm (US D) hook and A, ch23.
Row 1: Starting in second ch from hook, 1dc in back bump of each ch to end, turn. (*22 sts*)
Row 2: Ch1 (does not count as st), 1dc in each st, turn.
Rows 3–22: Rep Row 2.
Fasten off.

Edging
Round 1: Using a 2.5mm (US B-1 to C-2) hook and A, with RS facing join in yarn at centre bottom of square with a sl st, 1dc in same st, *1dc in each st to corner, 3dc in corner st, 1dc in each row-end to next corner, 3dc in corner st; rep from * once more, 1dc in each st to beg of round, sl st to join. Fasten off and sew in ends (see page 123).
Round 2: With RS facing, join B at centre bottom with a sl stBLO, *sl stBLO in each of next 2 sts, ch2; rep from * to beg of round, sl st to join.
Fasten off and sew in ends.

HEART
Using a 2.5mm (US B-1 to C-2) hook and Red, ch2.
Row 1: 2dc in second ch from hook, turn. (*2 sts*)
Row 2: Ch1 (does not count as st throughout), 2dc in next st, 1dc in last st, turn. (*3 sts*)
Row 3: Ch1, 2dc in next st, 1dc in next st, 2dc in next st, turn. (*5 sts*)
Row 4: Ch1, 2dc in next st, 1dc in each of next 3 sts, 2dc in next st, turn. (*7 sts*)
Row 5: Ch1, 2dc in next st, 1dc in each of next 5 sts, 2dc in next st, turn. (*9 sts*)
Row 6: Ch1, 2dc in next st, 1dc in each of next 3 sts, 2dc in next st, 1dc in each of next 3 sts, 2dc in next st, turn. (*12 sts*)
Row 7: Ch1, 2dc in next st, 1dc in each of next 3 sts, 2dc in next st, 1dc in each of next 2 sts, 2dc in next st, 1dc in each of next 3 sts, 2dc in next st, turn. (*16 sts*)
Rows 8 and 9: Ch1, 1dc in each st, turn.
Row 10: Ch1, 2dc in next st, 1dc in each of next 14 sts, 2dc in next st, turn. (*18 sts*)
Row 11: Ch1, 1dc in each st, turn.
Row 12: Ch1, 2dc in next st, 1dc in each of next 6 sts, 2dc in next st, 1dc in each of next 2 sts, 2dc in next st, 1dc in each of next 6 sts, 2dc in next st, turn. (*22 sts*)
Row 13: Ch1, 1dc in each st, turn.
Row 14: Ch1, 2dc in next st, 1dc in each of next 20 sts, 2dc in next st, turn. (*24 sts*)
Row 15: Ch1, 1dc in each st, turn.
Row 16: Ch1, 2dc in next st, 1dc in each of next 22 sts, 2dc in next st, turn. (*26 sts*)
Rows 17 and 18: Ch1, 1dc in each st, turn.

Right heart tip
Row 19: Ch1, 1dc in each of next 13 sts, leave rem sts unworked, turn.
Row 20: Ch1, dc2tog, 1dc in each of next 10 sts, 2dc in next st, turn. (*13 sts*)
Row 21: Ch1, 1dc in each of next 11 sts, dc2tog, turn. (*12 sts*)
Row 22: Ch1, dc2tog, 1dc in each of next 10 sts, turn. (*11 sts*)
Row 23: Ch1, dc2tog, 1dc in each of next 9 sts, turn. (*10 sts*)
Row 24: Ch1, dc2tog, 1dc in each of next 8 sts, turn. (*9 sts*)
Row 25: Ch1, dc2tog, 1dc in each of next 5 sts, dc2tog, turn. (*7 sts*)
Row 26: Ch1, dc2tog, 1dc in each of next 3 sts, dc2tog, turn. (*5 sts*)
Row 27: Ch1, dc2tog, 1dc in next st, dc2tog. (*3 sts*)
Fasten off.

Left heart tip
Row 28: Rejoin Red at centre of Row 18 with a sl st, 1dc in same st, 1dc in each st to end, turn.
Row 29: Ch1, 2dc in next st, 1dc in each of next 10 sts, dc2tog, turn. (*13 sts*)
Row 30: Ch1, dc2tog, 1dc in each of next 11 sts, turn. (*12 sts*)
Row 31: Ch1, 1dc in each of next 10 sts, dc2tog, turn. (*11 sts*)
Row 32: Ch1, dc2tog, 1dc in each of next 9 sts, turn. (*10 sts*)
Row 33: Ch1, dc2tog, 1dc in each of next 8 sts, turn. (*9 sts*)
Row 34: Ch1, dc2tog, 1dc in each of next 5 sts, dc2tog, turn. (*7 sts*)
Row 35: Ch1, dc2tog, 1dc in each of next 3 sts, dc2tog, turn. (*5 sts*)
Row 36: Ch1, dc2tog, 1dc in next st, dc2tog. (*3 sts*)
Fasten off.

Edging
Join in Red at centre bottom of heart, work dc all around edge of heart, working 2dc in 1 st if necessary when working around curves.
Fasten off.

FINISHING
Block the square (see page 123).
Using a sewing needle and thread, stitch the heart to the square, creating a 3-D effect as you sew. Leave a small part of the edging unsewn. Lightly stuff the heart to create a soft padded effect, then finish sewing the heart onto the square.

Whether it's a flat for one, a first home for two or that special forever home, there can be nothing more exciting than a new home. This idyllic little cottage with roses around the door makes the perfect greetings square, either as a card sent through the post or presented as a box frame picture.

new home cottage scene

SKILL RATING ● ○ ○

YARN AND MATERIALS

FOR THE BACKGROUND SQUARE:
Rowan Summerlite 4 ply (100% cotton), 4-ply (fingering) weight, 175m (191yd) per 50g (1¾oz) ball
- 1 ball of Duck Egg shade 419 (light turquoise) (A)
- Small amount of Mint shade 451 (light green) (B)

FOR THE COTTAGE:
Cascade Heritage (75% wool, 25% nylon), 4-ply (fingering) weight, 400m (437yd) per 100g (3½oz) skein (hank)
- Small amounts of:
- Limestone shade 5681 (beige)
- Camel shade 5610 (light brown)
- Cedar Green shade 5684 (dark green)
- Herb shade 5658 (green)
- Red shade 5607

Anchor Artiste Metallic (20% polyester, 80% viscose), 4-ply (fingering) weight, 100m (109yd) per 25g (⅞oz) ball
- Small amount of Gold shade 300

Tiny piece of toy stuffing

HOOK AND EQUIPMENT

3mm (US D) crochet hook

2.5mm (US B-1 to C-2) crochet hook

2mm (US steel size 4) crochet hook

Yarn needle

Blocking pins and mat

Fine-tipped black marker pen

Sewing needle and thread

TENSION (GAUGE)
Exact tension is not important for this project.

FINISHED MEASUREMENTS
9.5 x 9.5cm (3¾ x 3¾in)

ABBREVIATIONS
See page 127.

BACKGROUND SQUARE

Using a 3mm (US D) hook and A, ch23.
Row 1: Starting in second ch from hook, 1dc in back bump of each ch to end, turn. (*22 sts*)
Row 2: Ch1 (does not count as st), 1dc in each st, turn.
Rows 3–22: Rep Row 2.
Fasten off.

Edging
Round 1: Using a 2.5mm (US B-1 to C-2) hook and A, with RS facing join in yarn at centre bottom of square with a sl st, 1dc in same st, *1dc in each st to corner, 3dc in corner st, 1dc in each row-end to next corner, 3dc in corner st; rep from * once more, 1dc in each st to beg of round, sl st to join. Fasten off and sew in ends (see page 123).
Round 2: With RS facing, join B at centre bottom with a sl stBLO, *(1dcBLO, 1htrBLO) in next st, (1htrBLO, 1dcBLO) in next st, sl stBLO in each of next 2 sts; rep from * to beg of round, sl st to join.
Fasten off and sew in ends.

COTTAGE

Using a 2.5mm (US B-1 to C-2) hook and 2 strands of Limestone held together, ch17.
Row 1: Starting in second ch from hook, 1dc in back bump of each ch to end, turn. (*16 sts*)
Rows 2–10: Ch1 (does not count as st), 1dc in each st, turn.
Fasten off.

Edging
Round 1: Join 1 strand of Limestone in top right corner, *1dc in each st to corner, (1dc, ch2, 1dc) in corner st, 1dc in each row-end to next corner, (1dc, ch2, 1dc) in corner st; rep from * once more, sl st to join.
Fasten off.

ROOF
Using a 2.5mm (US B-1 to C-2) hook and 2 strands of Camel held together, ch20.
Row 1: Starting in third ch from hook, working in back bumps of chain, 1dc in each of next 16 ch, dc2tog, turn. (*17 sts*)
Row 2: Ch1 (does not count as st throughout), dc2tog, 1dc in each of next 13 sts, dc2tog, turn. (*15 sts*)
Row 3: Ch1, dc2tog, 1dc in each of next 11 sts, dc2tog, turn. (*13 sts*)
Row 4: Ch1, dc2tog, 1dc in each of next 9 sts, dc2tog, turn. (*11 sts*)
Row 5: Ch1, dc2tog, 1dc in each of next 7 sts, dc2tog, turn. (*9 sts*)
Row 6: Ch1, 1dc in each st.
Fasten off.

Edging
Round 1: Join 1 strand of Camel in top right corner, *1dc in each st to corner, (1dc, ch2, 1dc) in corner st, 1dc in each row-end to next corner, (1dc, ch2, 1dc) in corner st; rep from * once more, sl st to join.
Fasten off.

DOOR
Using 2mm (US steel size 4) hook and Cedar Green, ch7.
Row 1: Starting in second ch from hook, 1dc in back bump of each ch to end, turn. (*6 sts*)
Rows 2–6: Ch1 (does not count as st), 1dc in each st, turn.

Edging
Round 1: Join Cedar Green in top right corner, *1dc in each st to corner, (1dc, ch2, 1dc) in corner st, 1dc in each row-end to next corner, (1dc, ch2, 1dc) in corner st; rep from * once more, sl st to join.
Fasten off.

CHIMNEY
Using 2mm (US steel size 4) hook and Camel, ch4.
Row 1: Starting in second ch from hook, 1dc in back bump of each ch to end, turn. (*3 sts*)
Rows 2–6: Ch1 (does not count as st), 1dc in each st, turn.
Fasten off.
Roll rectangle into a tube and use yarn tail to secure.

FINISHING
Block the square (see page 123).

Using a sewing needle and thread stitch the roof onto the cottage. Stitch the door to the cottage, with the crochet rows positioned so that they run vertically from the top of the door to the bottom. Using a sewing needle and thread stitch the cottage to the square.

Using a fine-tipped black marker pen, draw on four small windows. Thread a length of Camel into a yarn needle and work straight stitches (see page 126) to frame the windows and add the panes.

Thread a length of Herb into a yarn needle and, using straight stitches, stitch the stems of the climbing rose onto the cottage, working around the windows and door. Use Red in the yarn needle to add French knots (see page 127) for the roses.

Use Gold in the yarn needle to sew a letter box and door handle onto the door.

Stitch the chimney to the top of the roof and tuck a tiny piece of toy stuffing into the opening of the chimney for smoke.

new home cottage scene

new home front door

New front door – new start! This square is perfect for making into a New Home greetings card and can even be personalised with the right house number. Quick to make and with the smallest amounts of yarn needed, this is a really fun make.

SKILL RATING ●●○

YARN AND MATERIALS

FOR THE BACKGROUND SQUARE:
Rowan Summerlite 4 ply (100% cotton), 4-ply (fingering) weight, 175m (191yd) per 50g (1¾oz) ball
   1 ball of Duck Egg shade 419 (light turquoise) (A)
   Small amount of Mint shade 451 (light green) (B)

FOR THE FRONT DOOR AND BAY TREES:
Cascade Heritage (75% wool, 25% nylon), 4-ply (fingering) weight, 400m (437yd) per 100g (3½oz) skein (hank)
   Small amounts of:
   Red shade 5607
   Camel shade 5610 (light brown)
   Cedar Green shade 5684 (dark green)
   Forged Iron shade 5736 (dark grey)

Anchor Artiste Metallic (20% polyester, 80% viscose), 4-ply (fingering) weight, 100m (109yd) per 25g (⅞oz) ball
   Gold shade 300

2 small straight twigs for the bay tree stems

Small amount of toy stuffing (optional)

HOOK AND EQUIPMENT
3mm (US D) crochet hook

2.5mm (US B-1 to C-2) crochet hook

2mm (US steel size 4) crochet hook

Yarn needle

Blocking pins and mat

Sewing needle and thread

Hot glue gun

Water-soluble coloured pencils to age pots (optional)

TENSION (GAUGE)
Exact tension is not important for this project.

FINISHED MEASUREMENTS
9.5 x 9.5cm (3¾ x 3¾in)

ABBREVIATIONS
See page 127.

BACKGROUND SQUARE

Using a 3mm (US D) hook and A, ch23.
Row 1: Starting in second ch from hook, 1dc in back bump of each ch to end, turn. (*22 sts*)
Row 2: Ch1 (does not count as st), 1dc in each st, turn.
Rows 3–22: Rep Row 2.
Fasten off.

Edging

Round 1: Using a 2.5mm (US B-1 to C-2) hook and A, with RS facing join in yarn at centre bottom of square with a sl st, 1dc in same st, *1dc in each st to corner, 3dc in corner st, 1dc in each row-end to next corner, 3dc in corner st; rep from * once more, 1dc in each st to beg of round, sl st to join.
Fasten off and sew in ends (see page 123).
Round 2: With RS facing, join B at centre bottom with a sl stBLO, *(1dcBLO, 1htrBLO) in next st, (1htrBLO, 1dcBLO) in next st, sl stBLO in each of next 2 sts; rep from * to beg of round, sl st to join.
Fasten off and sew in ends.

DOOR

Using a 2.5mm (US B-1 to C-2) hook and 2 strands of Red held together, ch15.
Row 1: Starting in second ch from hook, 1dc in back bump of each ch to end, turn. (*14 sts*)
Rows 2–10: Ch1 (does not count as st), 1dc in each st, turn.
Fasten off.

Edging

Round 1: Join 1 strand of Red in top right corner, *1dc in each st to corner, (1dc, ch2, 1dc) in corner st, 1dc in each row-end to next corner, (1dc, ch2, 1dc) in corner st; rep from * once more, sl st to join.
Fasten off.

POTS

(make 2)
Using a 2.5mm (US B-1 to C-2) hook and 2 strands of Camel held together, make a magic ring.
Row 1: (1dc, 2htr, 1dc) in ring to form a semi-circle. (*4 sts*)
Carefully close ring, keeping semi-circle shape and leaving a tiny opening for stem.
Fasten off.
Row 2: Rejoin 2 strands of Camel at beg of Row 1, 2dcBLO in first st, 1dcBLO in each of next 2 sts, 2dcBLO in last st, turn. (*6 sts*)
Row 3: Ch1 (does not count as st throughout), 1dc in each st, turn.
Row 4: Ch1, sl st in each st.
Fasten off.

TREES

(make 2)
Using 2mm (US steel size 4) and Cedar Green, make a magic ring.
Round 1: 8dc into ring. (*8 sts*)
Round 2: [1dc in next st, 2dc in next st] 4 times. (*12 sts*)
Round 3: 1dc in each st.
Round 4: [1dc in each of next 2 sts, 2dc in next st] 4 times. (*16 sts*)
Round 5: [1dc in next st, dc2tog] 5 times, 1dc in last st. (*11 sts*)
Add a small amount of toy stuffing if necessary to round out shape.
Work dc2tog until opening is closed and 1 st remains.
Fasten off.

FINISHING

Block the square (see page 123).
   Thread a length of Forged Iron in a yarn needle and stitch the panels onto the front door using running stitch (see page 126). Using a sewing needle and thread stitch the outside edge of the door to the square.
   Stitch the two pots either side of the front door, making sure to create the 3-D effect as you stitch them on. Use the water-soluble coloured pencils to add shading to the pots to age them.
   Push one of the twigs into the bottom of the tree ball for the stem, adding a touch of glue from a hot glue gun at the top of the twig before inserting. Repeat for the second tree. Insert each tree into a pot, adding glue from a hot glue gun to the bottom of the twig that will be inside the pot.
   Use a length of Gold in a yarn needle to stitch the house number, letter box and door handle onto the door. Use Red to stitch a small heart above the front door using small running stitches.
   Use Camel to stitch straight lines for a brick effect onto the background. Use the water-soluble coloured pencils to add shading to the brick wall if desired.

birthday present

The best things come in small packages and – while this present is not one to be opened – the sentiment that comes with this tiny square is just as good. Simply stick this square onto a greetings card mount for a unique and handmade birthday card.

SKILL RATING ● ○ ○

YARN AND MATERIALS
FOR THE BACKGROUND SQUARE:
Rowan Summerlite 4 ply (100% cotton), 4-ply (fingering) weight, 175m (191yd) per 50g (1¾oz) ball
  1 ball of Mustard shade 455 (A) (yellow)

Cascade Ultra Pima (100% cotton), DK (light worsted) weight, 200m (220yd) per 100g (3½oz) skein (hank)
  Small amount of White Asparagus shade 3835 (B) (off-white)

FOR THE PRESENT:
Cascade Heritage (75% wool, 25% nylon), 4-ply (fingering) weight, 400m (437yd) per 100g (3½oz) skein (hank)
  Small amounts of:
  Tutu shade 5613 (pink)
  Lemon shade 5644 (light yellow)

25cm (10in) of gold ribbon

Small piece of card for gift tag

Short length of gold string

HOOK AND EQUIPMENT
3mm (US-D) crochet hook

2.5mm (US B-1 to C-2) crochet hook

Yarn needle

Blocking pins and mat

Sewing needle and thread

TENSION (GAUGE)
Exact tension is not important for this project.

FINISHED MEASUREMENTS
9.5 x 9.5cm (3¾ x 3¾in)

ABBREVIATIONS
See page 127.

BACKGROUND SQUARE

Using a 3mm (US D) hook and A, ch23.
Row 1: Starting in second ch from hook, 1dc in back bump of each ch to end, turn. (*22 sts*)
Row 2: Ch1 (does not count as st), 1dc in each st, turn.
Rows 3–22: Rep Row 2.
Fasten off.

Edging
Round 1: Using a 2.5mm (US B-1 to C-2) hook and A, with RS facing join in yarn at centre bottom of square with a sl st, 1dc in same st, *1dc in each st to corner, 3dc in corner st, 1dc in each row-end to next corner, 3dc in corner st; rep from * once more, 1dc in each st to beg of round, sl st to join.
Fasten off and sew in ends (see page 123).
Round 2: With RS facing, join B at centre bottom with a sl stBLO, *2htrBLO in next st, sl stBLO in each of next 3 sts; rep from * to beg of round, sl st to join.
Fasten off and sew in ends.

PRESENT

Use 2 strands of Tutu held together throughout.
Using a 2.5mm (US B-1 to C-2) hook and 2 strands of Tutu held together, ch13.
Row 1: Starting in second ch from hook, 1dc in back bump of each ch to end, turn. (*12 sts*)
Rows 2–14: Ch1 (does not count as st), 1dc in each st, turn.
Fasten off.

Edging
Row 1: Join in 2 strands of Tutu at top left-hand corner with a sl st, 1dc in each row-end down left-hand side, ch2, 1dc in each st along bottom, ch2, 1dc in each row-end up right-hand side.
Fasten off and sew in ends.

Vertical stripes
Using a 2.5mm (US B-1 to C-2) hook and 1 strand of Lemon, work surface crochet in ridges on present.
Fasten off and sew in ends.

Top of present
Using a 2.5mm (US B-1 to C-2) hook and 2 strands of Tutu held together, ch16.
Row 1: Starting in second ch from hook, 1dc in back bump of each ch to end, turn. (*15 sts*)
Rows 2 and 3: Ch1 (does not count as st), 1dc in each st, turn.
Fasten off.
Join 2 strands of Tutu at the start of Row 3 with a sl stBLO, 1dcBLO in same st, 1dcBLO in each st to end, then work dc evenly down each short edge.
Fasten off.

FINISHING

Block the square (see page 123).
Position the present on the square. Cut a piece of ribbon 2–3cm (¾–1¼in) longer than the height of the present. Tuck one end under the centre bottom of the present, then using a sewing needle and thread stitch the present to the square securing the ribbon end at the same time.
Place the top of the present in position and tuck the other end of the ribbon under the top edge, then sew the top and ribbon in place. The top of the present should be a little proud of the surface.
Tie a bow in the remaining gold ribbon and sew it to the top of the present.
Cut out a tiny piece of card for a gift tag, punch a small hole near the top and thread the gold string through. Use the string to attach the tag to the ribbon.

birthday cupcake

Who doesn't love cake on their birthday and, when attached to a card mount, this miniature crochet cupcake makes the cheeriest of birthday greetings cards. Since the smallest amount of yarn is needed, this is the ideal make to use up all your leftover yarn.

SKILL RATING ● ○ ○

YARN AND MATERIALS

FOR THE BACKGROUND SQUARE:
Rowan Summerlite 4 ply (100% cotton), 4-ply (fingering) weight, 175m (191yd) per 50g (1¾oz) ball
   1 ball of Mustard shade 455 (A) (yellow)

Cascade Ultra Pima (100% cotton), DK (light worsted) weight, 200m (220yd) per 100g (3½oz) skein (hank)
   Small amount of White Asparagus shade 3835 (B) (off-white)

FOR THE CUPCAKE:
Cascade Heritage (75% wool, 25% nylon), 4-ply (fingering) weight, 400m (437yd) per 100g (3½oz) skein (hank)
   Small amounts of:
   Tutu shade 5613 (pink)
   Lemon shade 5644 (light yellow)
   White shade 5682

Anchor Artiste Metallic (20% polyester, 80% viscose), 4-ply (fingering) weight, 100m (109yd) per 25g (⅞oz) ball
   Small amount of Gold shade 300

Small amount of toy stuffing

Small birthday candle

Piece of gold card or gold pen

HOOK AND EQUIPMENT
3mm (US D) crochet hook
2.5mm (US B-1 to C-2) crochet hook
Yarn needle
Blocking pins and mat
Sewing needle and thread

TENSION (GAUGE)
Exact tension is not important for this project.

FINISHED MEASUREMENTS
9.5 x 9.5cm (3¾ x 3¾in)

ABBREVIATIONS
See page 127.

BACKGROUND SQUARE

Using a 3mm (US D) hook and A, ch23.
Row 1: Starting in second ch from hook, 1dc in back bump of each ch to end, turn. (*22 sts*)
Row 2: Ch1 (does not count as st), 1dc in each st, turn.
Rows 3–22: Rep Row 2.
Fasten off.

Edging

Round 1: Using a 2.5mm (US B-1 to C-2) hook and A, with RS facing join in yarn at centre bottom of square with a sl st, 1dc in same st, *1dc in each st to corner, 3dc in corner st, 1dc in each row-end to next corner, 3dc in corner st; rep from * once more, 1dc in each st to beg of round, sl st to join.
Fasten off and sew in ends (see page 123).
Round 2: With RS facing, join B at centre bottom with a sl stBLO, *2htrBLO in next st, sl stBLO in each of next 3 sts; rep from * to beg of round, sl st to join.
Fasten off and sew in ends.

CUPCAKE

Cake case base

Using a 2.5mm (US B-1 to C-2) hook and Tutu, make a magic ring.
Row 1: 8dc into ring. (*8 sts*)
Very loosely pull up ring to form a semi-circle, turn.
Row 2: Ch1 (does not count as st throughout), [2dc in next st] 8 times, turn. (*16 sts*)
Row 3: Ch1, [1dcBLO in next st, 2dcBLO in next st] 8 times. (*24 sts*)
Rows 4–7: Ch1, 1dc in each st, turn.
Row 8: Ch1, 1dc in each of next 6 sts, 2dc in next st, 1dc in each of next 10 sts, 2dc in next st, 1dc in each of next 6 sts, turn. (*26 sts*)
Rows 9 and 10: Ch1, 1dc in each st to end, turn.
Row 11: Ch1, sl stFLO in next st, *3trFLO in next st, sl stFLO in each of next 2 sts; rep from * to last st, 3trFLO in last st.
Fasten off Tutu.

Cake

Row 12: Using a 2.5mm (US B-1 to C-2) hook, join Lemon in unworked back loop at start of Row 11, 1dcBLO in each st, turn. (*26 sts*)
Rows 13–15: Ch1, 1dc in each st, turn.
Row 16: Ch1, [1dc in next st, dc2tog] 8 times, 1dc in each of next 2 sts, turn. (*18 sts*)
Row 17: Ch1, [dc2tog] 9 times, turn. (*9 sts*)
Rows 18–20: Ch1, 1dc in each st, turn.
Fasten off.

Icing

Using a 2.5mm (US B-1 to C-2) hook and White, ch81.
Row 1: Starting in second ch from hook, 2dc in each ch to end. (*160 sts*)
Fasten off.

FINISHING

Block the square (see page 123).
   Fold the edges of the cake case in to form the required shape, with sides sloping out from the base so that the case is widest at the top edge. Use a sewing needle and thread to stitch the cake case to the square.
   Sew the sides of the cake to the square and then lightly stuff case and cake so that the cupcake shape is formed. Leave an opening at the top of the cake for the candle to be inserted.
   Insert the candle into the top of the cake, cutting some of the bottom off if needed.
   Starting behind the candle to support it and allow it to stand straight, arrange the icing in swirls on top of the cake. Using a sewing needle and thread stitch the icing in place.
   Using short lengths of Gold, Tutu and A, sew sprinkles onto the icing.
   Either stick a small flame cut from gold card onto the back and front of the candle wick, or colour in the candle wick using the gold pen.

Nothing beats welcoming a new little one into the world and this square makes the perfect celebratory congratulations card when mounted on card and popped in the post. With just the smallest amounts of yarn being needed it is also great for using up all those leftover yarns tucked away in the cupboard.

baby's pram

SKILL RATING ● ○ ○

YARN AND MATERIALS
FOR THE BACKGROUND SQUARE:
Rowan Summerlite 4 ply (100% cotton), 4-ply (fingering) weight, 175m (191yd) per 50g (1¾oz) ball
   1 ball of Duck Egg shade 419 (light turquoise) (A)
   Small amount of Mustard shade 455 (yellow) (B)

FOR THE PRAM AND BABY:
Cascade Ultra Pima (100% cotton), DK (light worsted) weight, 200m (220yd) per 100g (3½oz) skein (hank)
   Small amounts of:
   Rich Gold shade 3866 (golden yellow)
   Buff shade 3719 (light brown)

Cascade Heritage (75% wool, 25% nylon), 4-ply (fingering) weight, 400m (437yd) per 100g (3½oz) skein (hank)
   Small amounts of:
   Chanterelle shade 5751 (pink)
   Lemon shade 5644 (light yellow)
   Forged Iron shade 5736 (dark grey)

Pair of small black safety eyes

HOOK AND EQUIPMENT
3mm (US D) crochet hook
2.5mm (US B-1 to C-2) crochet hook
2mm (US steel size 4) crochet hook
Yarn needle
Blocking pins and mat
Sewing needle and thread
Pink water-soluble coloured pencil

TENSION (GAUGE)
Exact tension is not important for this project.

FINISHED MEASUREMENTS
9.5 x 9.5 cm (3¾ x 3¾in)

ABBREVIATIONS
See page 127.

BACKGROUND SQUARE
Using a 3mm (US D) hook and A, ch25.
Row 1: Starting in second ch from hook, 1dc in back bump of each ch to end, turn. (*24 sts*)
Row 2: Ch1 (does not count as st), 1dc in each st, turn.
Rows 3–25: Rep Row 2.
Fasten off.

Edging
Round 1: Using a 2.5mm (US B-1 to C-2) hook and A, with RS facing join in yarn at centre bottom of square with a sl st, 1dc in same st, *1dc in each st to corner, 3dc in corner st, 1dc in each row-end to next corner, 3dc in corner st; rep from * once more, 1dc in each st to beg of round, sl st to join. Fasten off and sew in ends (see page 123).
Round 2: With RS facing, join B at centre bottom with a sl stBLO, *(sl stBLO, ch2, sl stBLO) in next st, sl stBLO in next st; rep from * to beg of round, sl st to join.
Fasten off and sew in ends.

PRAM
Using a 2.5mm (US B-1 to C-2) hook and Rich Gold, ch16.
Row 1: Starting in second ch from hook, 1dc in back bump of each ch to end, turn. (*15 sts*)
Row 2: Ch1 (does not count as st throughout), dc2tog, 1dc in each of next 11 sts, dc2tog, turn. (*13 sts*)
Row 3: Ch1, dc2tog, 1dc in each of next 9 sts, dc2tog, turn. (*11 sts*)
Row 4: Ch1, dc2tog, 1dc in each of next 7 sts, dc2tog, turn. (*9 sts*)
Row 5: Ch1, dc2tog, 1dc in each of next 5 sts, dc2tog, turn. (*7 sts*)
Row 6: Ch1, dc2tog, 1dc in each of next 3 sts, dc2tog, turn. (*5 sts*)
Row 7: Ch1, dc2tog, 1dc in next st, dc2tog. (*3 sts*)
Fasten off.

PRAM HOOD

Using a 2.5mm (US B-1 to C-2) hook and Rich Gold, ch7.
Row 1: Starting in second ch from hook, 1dc in back bump of each ch to end, turn. (*6 sts*)
Row 2: Ch1 (does not count as st throughout), 1dc in each st, turn.
Row 3: Ch1, dc2tog, 1dc in each of next 4 sts, turn. (*5 sts*)
Row 4: Ch1, 1dc in each of next 3 sts, dc2tog, turn. (*4 sts*)
Row 5: Ch1, 1dc in each st, turn.
Row 6: Ch1, 1dc in each of next 2 sts, dc2tog, turn. (*3 sts*)
Row 7: Ch1, dc2tog, 1dc in next st. (*2 sts*)
Fasten off.

Edging

Working on WS, stitch hood to pram base.
Round 1: Join in Rich Gold at base of hood, 1dc in each st or row end around the pram base, working 2dc into 1 st if needed around curves. At right-hand corner of top edge of pram base, ch2, then 1dc in each st along top edge of pram base, then up front edge and around top of hood to beg of round, sl st to join.
Round 2: Starting at beg of round, work a row of sl st surface crochet from the back of the hood to the centre of the pram base edge.
Fasten off.

WHEELS

Using a 2.5mm (US B-1 to C-2) hook and Buff, make a magic ring.
Round 1: 4dc into ring. (*4 sts*)
Round 2: 2dc in each st, sl st to join. (*8 sts*)
Fasten off.

BABY

Using a 2.5mm (US B-1 to C-2) hook and Peach Pearl, make a magic ring.
Round 1: 6dc into ring. (*6 sts*)
Round 2: 2dc in each st. (*12 sts*)
Round 3: [1dc in next st, 2dc in next st] 6 times. (*18 sts*)
Rounds 4 and 5: 1dc in each st.
Round 6: [1dc in next st, dc2tog] 6 times. (*12 sts*)
Round 7: [1dc in next st, dc2tog] 4 times. (*8 sts*)
Fasten off.

FINISHING

Block the square (see page 123).

Using a sewing needle and thread, stitch the outside edge of the pram to the square, creating a 3-D effect to the pram as you sew.

Insert the two safety eyes or work French knots (see page 127) for eyes on the baby. Using Lemon sew a couple of curls for the hair. Colour rosy cheeks with a water-soluble coloured pencil. Insert the baby's head behind the pram hood so that the neck is hidden and the face is peeping out. Sew in place.

Stitch the pram wheels in place.

Using Forged Iron sew a loop at the end of the pram for the handle, then sew two straight stitches (see page 126) to form the cross-bar frame of the pram, with the ends going through the centre of the wheels. Work a French knot in each wheel centre.

Whether mounted on a greetings card or displayed in a box picture frame as a Christening present, this simple square can be worked in any colourway to suit.`

new baby in a basket

SKILL RATING ●●○

YARN AND MATERIALS

FOR THE BACKGROUND SQUARE:
Rowan Summerlite 4 ply (100% cotton), 4-ply (fingering) weight, 175m (191yd) per 50g (1¾oz) ball
- 1 ball of Duck Egg shade 419 (light turquoise) (A)
- Small amount of Mustard shade 455 (yellow) (B)

FOR THE BASKET, BABY AND BALLOONS:
Cascade Ultra Pima (100% cotton), DK (light worsted) weight, 200m (220yd) per 100g (3½oz) skein (hank)
- Small amount of Rich Gold shade 3866 (golden yellow)

Cascade Heritage (75% wool, 25% nylon), 4-ply (fingering) weight, 400m (437yd) per 100g (3½oz) skein (hank)
- Small amounts of:
  Camel shade 5610 (light brown)
  White shade 5682
  Mustard shade 5652 (dark yellow)
  Lemon shade 5644 (light yellow)
  Forged Iron shade 5736 (dark grey)

Pair of small black safety eyes

HOOK AND EQUIPMENT
3mm (US D) crochet hook
2.5mm (US B-1 to C-2) crochet hook
Yarn needle
Blocking pins and mat
Sewing needle and thread
Pink water-soluble coloured pencil
Small amount of toy stuffing

TENSION (GAUGE)
Exact tension is not important for this project.

FINISHED MEASUREMENTS
9.5 x 9.5cm (3¾ x 3¾in)

ABBREVIATIONS
See page 127.

BACKGROUND SQUARE
Using a 3mm (US D) hook and A, ch25.
Row 1: Starting in second ch from hook, 1dc in back bump of each ch to end, turn. (*24 sts*)
Row 2: Ch1 (does not count as st), 1dc in each st, turn.
Rows 3–25: Rep Row 2.
Fasten off.

Edging
Round 1: Using a 2.5mm (US B-1 to C-2) hook and A, with RS facing join in yarn at centre bottom of square with a sl st, 1dc in same st, *1dc in each st to corner, 3dc in corner st, 1dc in each row-end to next corner, 3dc in corner st; rep from * once more, 1dc in each st to beg of round, sl st to join.
Fasten off and sew in ends (see page 123).
Round 2: With RS facing, join B at centre bottom with a sl stBLO, *(sl stBLO, ch2, sl stBLO) in next st, sl stBLO in next st; rep from * to beg of round, sl st to join.
Fasten off and sew in ends.

BASKET
Using a 2.5mm (US B-1 to C-2) hook and Rich Gold, ch7.
Row 1: Starting in second ch from hook, 1dc in back bump of each ch to end, turn. (*6 sts*)
Row 2: Ch1 (does not count as st throughout), 2dc in next st, 1dc in next st, 2dc in each of next 2 sts, 1dc in next st, 2dc in next st, turn. (*10 sts*)
Rows 3 and 4: Ch1, 1dc in each st, turn.
Row 5: Ch1, 2dc in next st, 1dc in each of next 8 sts, 2dc in next st, turn. (*12 sts*)

Row 6: Ch1, 2dc in next st, 1dc in each of next 4 sts, 2dc in next st, 1dc in each of next 5 sts, 2dc in next st, turn. (*15 sts*)
Rows 7 and 8: Ch1, 1dc in each st, turn.
Row 9: Ch1, 2dc in next st, 1dc in each of next 13 sts, 2dc in next st. (*17 sts*)
Fasten off.

Edging
With RS facing, join in Rich Gold at left-hand corner of top edge, work crab st all along top edge. Fasten off.

BABY
Using a 2.5mm (US B-1 to C-2) hook and Camel, make a magic ring.
Round 1: 6dc into ring. (*6 sts*)
Round 2: 2dc in each st. (*12 sts*)
Round 3: [1dc in next st, 2dc in next st] 6 times. (*18 sts*)
Round 4: [1dc in each of next 2 sts, 2dc in next st] 6 times. (*24 sts*)
Round 5: 1dc in each st.
Round 6: [1dc in each of next 2 sts, dc2tog] 6 times. (*18 sts*)
Insert safety eyes or work 2 French knots (see page 127).
Round 7: [1dc in next st, dc2tog] 6 times. (*12 sts*)
Round 8: [1dc in each of next 4 sts, dc2tog] twice. (*10 sts*)
Round 9: 1dc in each st.
Round 10: [1dc in next st, 2dc in next st] 5 times. (*15 sts*)
Rounds 11–13: 1dc in each st.
Round 14: [Dc2tog, 1dc in next st] 5 times. (*10 sts*)
Rounds 15 and 16: 1dc in each st.
Fasten off.
Stuff baby very lightly and stitch up at base.

BLANKET
Using a 2.5mm (US B-1 to C-2) hook and White, ch18.
Row 1: Starting in second ch from hook, 1dc in each ch to end, turn. (*17 sts*)
Rows 2–10: Ch1 (does not count as st throughout), 1dc in each st, turn.
Row 11: [Ch1, sl st in next st] to end.
Fasten off and sew in ends.

LARGE BALLOON
Using a 2.5mm (US B-1 to C-2) hook and Mustard, make a magic ring.
Round 1: 6dc into ring. (*6 sts*)
Round 2: 2dc in each st. (*12 sts*)
Round 3: [1dc in next st, 2dc in next st] 6 times. (*18 sts*)
Round 4: [1dc in each of next 2 sts, 2dc in next st] 6 times. (*24 sts*)
Rounds 5 and 6: 1dc in each st.
Round 7: Dc2tog, 1dc in each of next 10 sts, dc2tog, 1dc in each of next 10 sts. (*22 sts*)
Round 8: Dc2tog, 1dc in each of next 9 sts, dc2tog, 1dc in each of next 9 sts. (*20 sts*)
Round 9: [1dc in each of next 3 sts, dc2tog] 4 times. (*16 sts*)
Round 10: [1dc in each of next 2 sts, dc2tog] 4 times. (*12 sts*)
Round 11: [Dc2tog] 6 times. (*6 sts*)
Round 12: Dc2tog, 1dc in each of next 2 sts, dc2tog. (*4 sts*)
Round 13: 1dc in each st, sl st to join.
Fasten off.

SMALL BALLOONS
(make 1 in Mustard, 2 in Lemon)
Using a 2.5mm (US B-1 to C-2) hook and Mustard or Lemon, make a magic ring.
Round 1: 4dc into ring. (*4 sts*)
Round 2: 2dc in each st. (*8 sts*)
Round 3: [1dc in next st, 2dc in next st] 4 times. (*12 sts*)
Round 4: [1dc in each of next 2 sts, 2dc in next st] 4 times. (*16 sts*)
Rounds 5–8: 1dc in each st.
Round 9: [1dc in each of next 2 sts, dc2tog] 4 times. (*12 sts*)
Round 10: [Dc2tog] 6 times. (*6 sts*)
Round 11: [Dc2tog] 3 times. (*3 sts*)
Round 12: 1dc in each st, sl st to join.
Fasten off.

FINISHING
Block the square (see page 123).

Using a sewing needle and thread, stitch the outside edge of the basket to the square, creating a 3-D effect as you sew.

Wrap the baby in the blanket and stitch the blanket edges together at the back. Place the baby into the basket and sew in place. Use Forged Iron to sew a couple of loops on top of the baby's head for hair.

Tie a string onto each balloon in the contrasting yellow and use the yarn tails to stitch them to the sides of the basket. Add a small yarn bow to each side of the blanket and sew in place.

Stitch the balloons in place.

chapter 3
celebration squares

Any self-respecting Easter Rabbit needs a flower crown full of spring flowers, and whether added to a spring blanket or cushion, spring bunting or an Easter card, this bright and sunny square will certainly bring a smile.

easter rabbit

SKILL RATING ● ● ●

YARN AND MATERIALS

FOR THE BACKGROUND SQUARE:
Rowan Summerlite 4 ply (100% cotton), 4-ply (fingering) weight, 175m (191yd) per 50g (1¾oz) ball
  1 ball of Buttermilk shade 421 (light yellow) (A)
  Small amount of Mint shade 451 (light green) (B)

FOR THE RABBIT AND FLOWER CROWN:
Cascade Heritage (75% wool, 25% nylon), 4-ply (fingering) weight, 400m (437yd) per 100g (3½oz) skein (hank)
  Small amounts of:
  Camel shade 5610 (light brown)
  Herb shade 5658 (green)
  Golden Yellow shade 5752 (dark yellow)
  Mustard shade 5652 (yellow)
  Forged Iron shade 5736 (dark grey)
  Chanterelle shade 5751 (pink)

Pair of small black safety eyes

HOOK AND EQUIPMENT

3mm (US D) crochet hook
2.5mm (US B-1 to C-2) crochet hook
2mm (US steel size 4) crochet hook
Yarn needle
Blocking pins and mat
Sewing needle and thread
Pink water-soluble coloured pencil

TENSION (GAUGE)

Exact tension is not important for this project.

FINISHED MEASUREMENTS

9.5 x 9.5cm (3¾ x 3¾in)

ABBREVIATIONS

See page 127.

BACKGROUND SQUARE

Using a 3mm (US D) hook and A, ch25.
Row 1: Starting in second ch from hook, 1dc in back bump of each ch to end, turn. (*24 sts*)
Row 2: Ch1 (does not count as st), 1dc in each st, turn.
Rows 3–25: Rep Row 2.
Fasten off.

Edging

Round 1: Using a 2.5mm (US B-1 to C-2) hook and A, with RS facing join in yarn at centre bottom of square with a sl st, 1dc in same st, *1dc in each st to corner, 3dc in corner st, 1dc in each row-end to next corner, 3dc in corner st; rep from * once more, 1dc in each st to beg of round, sl st to join. Fasten off and sew in ends (see page 123).
Round 2: With RS facing, join B at centre bottom with a sl stBLO, *3htrBLO in next st, sl stBLO in each of next 3 sts; rep from * to beg of round, sl st to join.
Fasten off and sew in ends.

RABBIT

Using a 2.5mm (US B-1 to C-2) hook and 2 strands of Camel held together, ch11.
Row 1: Starting in second ch from hook, 1dc in each ch to end, turn. (*10 sts*)
Row 2: Ch1 (does not count as st throughout), 2dc in first st, 1dc in each st to last st, 2dc in last st, turn. (*12 sts*)
Row 3: Ch1, 2dc in first st, 1dc in each st to last st, 2dc in last st, turn. (*14 sts*)

TIP
As you work the edging round you will find that the head starts to slightly curve inwards. This will add to the 3-D effect when you stitch the head to the square.

With RS facing, miss 4 sts along top edge of head and join in 2 strands of Camel held together with a sl st in next st, 1dc in same st, 1dc in each of next 2 sts, turn. Rep Rows 14–21.

Edging
With RS facing, using a 2.5mm (US B-1 to C-2) hook, join 1 strand of Camel at centre of bottom with a sl st, 1dc in same st, 1dc in each st and row end around head and ears, sl st to join.
Fasten off and sew in ends.

FLOWER CROWN
For the band:
Using a 2mm (US steel size 4) hook and Herb, ch18.
Row 1: Starting in second ch from hook, sl st in each ch to end. Fasten off.

For the flowers:
(make 2 in Golden Yellow, 1 in Mustard)
Using a 2mm (US steel size 4) hook, make a magic ring.
Round 1: *Sl st into ring, ch3, starting in second ch from hook, sl st in each of next 2 ch, sl st into ring; rep from * 4 times. (*5 petals*)
Fasten off and pull up magic ring to close.
Work a French knot (see page 127) in other yellow into each flower.

FINISHING
Block the square (see page 123).
Attach the safety eyes to the rabbit head or work 2 French knots using Forged Iron. Stitch on the nose with Forged Iron.
Using Peach Pearl, work some long satin stitches (see page 127) on the inside of the ears.
Using a sewing needle and thread stitch the head to the square, creating a 3-D effect for the head as you sew. Using the pink water-soluble coloured pencil shade two rosy cheeks on the head.
Stitch the flower crown band around the top of the head at the base of the ears. Stitch the flowers to the band. Using Herb work some short straight stitches (see page 126) for leaves. Work some French knots in each of the yellows for buds.

Row 4: Ch1, 2dc in first st, 1dc in each st to last st, 2dc in last st, turn. (*16 sts*)
Rows 5–7: Ch1, 1dc in each st, turn.
Row 8: Ch1, dc2tog, 1dc in each st to last 2 sts, dc2tog, turn. (*14 sts*)
Row 9: Ch1, dc2tog, 1dc in each st to last 2 sts, dc2tog, turn. (*12 sts*)
Row 10: Ch1, 1dc in each st, turn.
Row 11: Ch1, dc2tog, 1dc in each st to last 2 sts, dc2tog, turn. (*10 sts*)
Row 12: Ch1, 1dc in each st, turn.
Row 13: Ch1, 1dc in each of next 3 sts, leave rem sts unworked, turn.
Row 14: Ch1, 1dc in next st, 2dc in next st, 1dc in next st, turn. (*4 sts*)
Row 15: Ch1, 1dc in each st, turn.
Row 16: Ch1, 1dc in next st, 2dc in next st, 1dc in each of next 2 sts, turn. (*5 sts*)
Row 17: Ch1, 1dc in next st, dc2tog, 1dc in each of next 2 sts, turn. (*4 sts*)
Row 18: Ch1, 1dc in next st, dc2tog, 1dc in next st, turn. (*3 sts*)
Row 19: Ch1, 1dc in each st, turn.
Row 20: Ch1, 1dc in next st, dc2tog, turn. (*2 sts*)
Row 21: Ch1, dc2tog.
Fasten off.

This square, with its spring bird sat keeping its eggs warm, makes a beautiful Easter greetings card or a square to be added into some spring bunting. The nest is decorated with a few tiny twigs to give a subtle 3-D effect, with the bird also sitting slightly proud of the background.

easter nest

SKILL RATING ●●●

YARN AND MATERIALS

FOR THE BACKGROUND SQUARE:
Rowan Summerlite 4 ply (100% cotton), 4-ply (fingering) weight, 175m (191yd) per 50g (1¾oz) ball
- 1 ball of Buttermilk shade 421 (light yellow) (A)
- Small amount of Mint shade 451 (light green) (B)

FOR THE BIRD AND NEST:
Cascade Heritage (75% wool, 25% nylon,), 4-ply (fingering) weight, 400m (437yd) per 100g (3½oz) skein (hank)
- Small amounts of:
- Camel shade 5610 (light brown)
- Limestone shade 5681 (beige)
- Golden Yellow shade 5752 (dark yellow)
- Mustard shade 5652 (yellow)
- Cinnamon shade 5640 (reddish brown)
- Herb shade 5658 (green)

FOR THE EGGS:
Rowan Summerlite 4 ply (100% cotton), 4-ply (fingering) weight, 175m (191yd) per 50g (1¾oz) ball
- Small amount of Duck Egg shade 419 (light turquoise)

Small black safety eye
Small twigs (optional)

HOOK AND EQUIPMENT
3mm (US D) crochet hook
2.5mm (US B-1 to C-2) crochet hook
2mm (US steel size 4) crochet hook
Yarn needle
Blocking pins and mat
Sewing needle and thread
Hot glue gun
Yellow water-soluble coloured pencil

TENSION (GAUGE)
Exact tension is not important for this project.

FINISHED MEASUREMENTS
9.5 x 9.5cm (3¾ x 3¾in)

ABBREVIATIONS
See page 127.

BACKGROUND SQUARE
Using a 3mm (US D) hook and A, ch25.
Row 1: Starting in second ch from hook, 1dc in back bump of each ch to end, turn. (*24 sts*)
Row 2: Ch1 (does not count as st), 1dc in each st, turn.
Rows 3–25: Rep Row 2.
Fasten off.

Edging
Round 1: Using a 2.5mm (US B-1 to C-2) hook and A, with RS facing join in yarn at centre bottom of square with a sl st, 1dc in same st, *1dc in each st to corner, 3dc in corner st, 1dc in each row-end to next corner, 3dc in corner st; rep from * once more, 1dc in each st to beg of round, sl st to join. Fasten off and sew in ends (see page 123).
Round 2: With RS facing, join B at centre bottom with a sl stBLO, *3htrBLO in next st, sl stBLO in each of next 3 sts; rep from * to beg of round, sl st to join.
Fasten off and sew in ends.

BIRD
Using a 2.5mm (US B-1 to C-2) hook and 1 strand of Camel and 1 strand of Limestone held together, ch16.
Row 1: Starting in second ch from hook, 1dc in each ch to end, turn. (*15 sts*)
Row 2: Ch1 (does not count as st throughout), 2dc in first st, 1dc in each st to last 2 sts, dc2tog, turn.
Row 3: Ch1, sl st in each of next 3 sts, 1dc in each st to last 2 sts, dc2tog, turn. (*11 sts not incl sl sts*)
Row 4: Ch1, dc2tog, 1dc in each of next 7 sts, dc2tog, turn. (*9 sts*)
Row 5: Ch1, dc2tog, 1dc in each of next 5 sts, dc2tog, turn. (*7 sts*)
Row 6: Ch1, dc2tog, 1dc in each of next 3 sts, dc2tog, turn. (*5 sts*)
Row 7: Ch1, dc2tog, 1dc, dc2tog. (*3 sts*)
Fasten off.

TIP
As you work the edging round you will find that the bird starts to slightly curve inwards. This will add to the 3-D effect when you stitch the bird to the square.

Edging
Round 1: With RS facing, using a 2.5mm (US B-1 to C-2) hook, join Camel at centre of bottom with a sl st, 1dc in same st, 1dc in each st around bird, working 2dc in sts around curves, to beg of round, sl st to join.
Round 2: Ch1 (does not count as st), 1dc in each st around bird, working 2dc in sts around curves, to beg of round, sl st to join.
Fasten off and sew in ends.

Tail
Using a 2.5mm (US B-1 to C-2) hook and 1 strand of Golden Yellow and 1 strand of Mustard held together, join in yarn at narrow end of body for tail, 3trBLO in each of next 3 sts.
Fasten off and sew in ends.

WING
Using a 2.5mm (US B-1 to C-2) hook and Mustard, ch7.
Round 1: Starting in second ch from hook, 1dc in each ch to last ch, 3dc in next ch, working down opposite side of ch, 1dc in each ch to beg, ch1 across bottom of chain, sl st to join. (*13 sts*)
Fasten off Mustard.
Round 2: Join in Golden Yellow, 1dcBLO in each of next 5 sts, 2dcBLO in each of next 3 sts around curve, 1dcBLO in each st to end, ch1 across bottom, sl st to join. (*16 sts*)
Fasten off Golden Yellow.
Round 3: Join in Mustard, 1dcBLO in each of next 7 sts, 2dcBLO in each of next 2 sts around curve, 1dcBLO in each st to end, ch1 across bottom, sl st to join. (*18 sts*)
Fasten off Mustard.
Round 4: Join in Golden Yellow, 1dcBLO in each of next 9 sts, 2dcBLO in each of next 2 sts around curve, 1dcBLO in each st to end, ch1 across bottom, sl st to join. (*20 sts*)
Fasten off and sew in ends.
Using 1 strand of Golden Yellow, work a line of sl st surface crochet up centre of wing.
Fasten off.

BEAK
Using a 2mm (US steel size 4) hook and Golden Yellow, ch2.
Row 1: 2dc in second ch from hook, turn. (*2 sts*)
Row 2: Ch1 (does not count as st throughout), 2dc in each st, turn. (*4 sts*)
Row 3: Ch1, 1dc in each st.
Fasten off.

NEST
Using 2.5mm (US B-1 to C-2) hook and Cinnamon, ch23.
Row 1: Starting in second ch from hook, sl st in next ch, 1dc in each ch to last ch, sl st in next ch, turn. (*20 sts not incl sl sts*)
Row 2: Ch1 (does not count as st), sl st in each st to end.
Fasten off.

EGGS
(make 3)
Using a 2mm (US steel size 4) hook and Duck Egg, make a magic ring.
Round 1: 4dc into ring.
Round 2: [1dc in next st, 2dc in next st] twice. (*6 sts*)
Rounds 3 and 4: 1dc in each st.
Round 5: Dc2tog, 1dc in each st. (*4 sts*)
Fasten off and close up.

LEAVES
(make 5)
Using a 2.5mm (US B-1 to C-2) hook and Herb, ch5.
Row 1: Starting in second ch from hook, sl st in next ch, 1dc in next ch, 1htr in next ch, 1dc in next ch.
Fasten off.

FINISHING
Block the square (see page 123).
   Attach the safety eye to the bird's head or sew a French knot (see page 127) for the eye.
   Fold beak in half to make a pointed beak and stitch closed.
   Sew the wing and beak onto the bird.
   Sew or stick the nest to the square. Stick the twigs onto the nest. Sew or stick the leaves around the bottom of the nest. Stick or sew the eggs in to the nest. Place the bird on top of the eggs and nest and stitch into place, creating a 3-D effect to the bird as you sew. If needed, add a little shading around the edges of the bird using the yellow water-soluble coloured pencil.

While this little diya lamp is made out of yarn rather than clay, it will still shine brightly during Diwali. Bright colours and gold yarn add to the celebratory feel of this square, whether sent as a greetings card or framed in a small box picture frame.

diwali candle

SKILL RATING ● ○ ○

YARN AND MATERIALS

FOR THE BACKGROUND SQUARE:
Rowan Summerlite 4 ply (100% cotton), 4-ply (fingering) weight, 175m (191yd) per 50g (1¾oz) ball
- 1 ball of Aqua shade 433 (turquoise) (A)
- Small amount of Mustard shade 455 (yellow) (B)

FOR THE DIYA LAMP AND FLAME:
Cascade Heritage (75% wool, 25% nylon), 4-ply (fingering) weight, 400m (437yd) per 100g (3½oz) skein (hank)
- Small amounts of:
- Tutu shade 5613 (pink)
- Golden Yellow shade 5752 (dark yellow)
- Herb shade 5658 (green)
- Royal shade 5615 (blue)

Anchor Artiste Metallic (20% polyester, 80% viscose), 4-ply (fingering) weight, 100m (109yd) per 25g (⅞oz) ball
- Small amount of Gold shade 0300

Small beads/sequins/stars

HOOK AND EQUIPMENT

3mm (US D) crochet hook

2.5mm (US B-1 to C-2) crochet hook

2mm (US steel size 4) crochet hook

Yarn needle

Blocking pins and mat

Sewing needle and thread

TENSION (GAUGE)
Exact tension is not important for this project.

FINISHED MEASUREMENTS
9.5 x 9.5cm (3¾ x 3¾in)

ABBREVIATIONS
See page 127.

BACKGROUND SQUARE
Using a 3mm (US D) hook and A, ch25.
Row 1: Starting in second ch from hook, 1dc in back bump of each ch to end, turn. (*24 sts*)
Row 2: Ch1 (does not count as st), 1dc in each st, turn.
Rows 3-25: Rep Row 2.
Fasten off.

Edging
Round 1: Using a 2.5mm (US B-1 to C-2) hook and A, with RS facing join in yarn at centre bottom of square with a sl st, 1dc in same st, *1dc in each st to corner, 3dc in corner st, 1dc in each row-end to next corner, 3dc in corner st; rep from * once more, 1dc in each st to beg of round, sl st to join. Fasten off and sew in ends (see page 123).
Round 2: With RS facing, join B at centre bottom with a sl stBLO, *(sl stBLO, ch2, sl stBLO) in next st, sl stBLO in next st; rep from * to beg of round, sl st to join. Fasten off and sew in ends.

DIYA LAMP
Using a 2.5mm (US B-1 to C-2) hook and 2 strands of Tutu held together, make a magic ring.
Round 1: 4dc into ring. (*4 sts*)
Round 2: 2dc in each st. (*8 sts*)
Round 3: 2dc in each st. (*16 sts*)
Round 4: [1dc in next st, 2dc in next st] 8 times. (*24 sts*)
Round 5: 1dc in each st.
Round 6: [1dc in each of next 2 sts, 1htr in each of next 2 sts, 1tr in each of next 4 sts, 1htr in each of next 2 sts, 1dc in each of next 2 sts] twice, sl st to join.
Fasten off.

Round 7: Join in 2 strands of Golden Yellow held together, [1dcBLO in each of next 5 sts, 2dcBLO in next st] 4 times, sl st to join. (*28 sts*)
Fasten off.
Round 8: Join in 2 strands of Herb held together, [1dcBLO in each of next 3 sts, 2dcBLO in next st] 7 times, sl st to join. (*35 sts*)
Fasten off.
Round 9: Join in 2 strands of Royal held together, [1dcBLO in each of next 4 sts, 2dcBLO in next st] 4 times, 1htrBLO in next st, 1trBLO in next st, ch2, sl stBLO in second ch from hook, 1trBLO in next st, 1htrBLO in next st, 2dcBLO in next st, [1dcBLO in each of next 4 sts, 2dcBLO in next st] twice, sl st to join.
Fasten off and sew in ends.

FLAME

Using a 2mm (US steel size 4) hook and 2 strands of Golden Yellow held together, make a magic ring.
Round 1: 4dc into ring. (*4 sts*)
Round 2: [1dc in next st, 2dc in next st] twice. (*6 sts*)
Round 3: 1dc in each st.
Round 4: [1dc in each of next 2 sts, 2dc in next st] twice. (*8 sts*)
Round 5: 1dc in each st.
Round 6: [1dc in each of next 2 sts, dc2tog] twice. (*6 sts*)
Use yarn tail to close up top of flame to a point.

FINISHING

Block the square (see page 123).

Using a yarn needle and either the coloured yarns or Gold, decorate the lamp with small running stitches and French knots (see pages 126 and 127). Add Gold straight stitches from the base of the flame to the tip.

Fold the back of the lamp in towards the centre to create a flat back and a curved front. Stitch the lamp to the square keeping the curved 3-D effect as you sew.

Decorate the rest of the square with beads/stars/sequins and French knots.

This square celebrating Hanukkah could not be simpler to make, because the nine branches of the candelabra are all created with simple crochet chains. Quick and easy to complete, it will shine brightly when on display.

hanukkah candelabra

SKILL RATING ● ○ ○

YARN AND MATERIALS
FOR THE BACKGROUND SQUARE:
Rowan Summerlite 4 ply (100% cotton), 4-ply (fingering) weight, 175m (191yd) per 50g (1¾oz) ball
   1 ball of Aqua shade 433 (turquoise) (A)
   Small amount of Mustard shade 455 (yellow) (B)

FOR THE CANDELABRA AND FLAMES:
Anchor Artiste Metallic (80% viscose, 20% polyester), 4-ply (fingering) weight, 100m (109yd) per 25g (⅞oz) ball
   Small amount of Gold shade 0300

Cascade Heritage (75% wool, 25% nylon), 4-ply (fingering) weight, 400m (437yd) per 100g (3½oz) skein (hank)
   Small amounts of:
   Golden Yellow shade 5752 (dark yellow)
   Royal shade 5615 (blue)

HOOK AND EQUIPMENT
3mm (US D) crochet hook
2.5mm (US B-1 to C-2) crochet hook
2mm (US steel size 4) hook crochet hook
Yarn needle
Blocking pins and mat
Sewing needle and thread
Pins

TENSION (GAUGE)
Exact tension is not important for this project.

FINISHED MEASUREMENTS
9.5 x 9.5cm (3¾ x 3¾in)

ABBREVIATIONS
See page 127.

BACKGROUND SQUARE
Using a 3mm (US D) hook and A, ch25.
Row 1: Starting in second ch from hook, 1dc in back bump of each ch to end, turn. (*24 sts*)
Row 2: Ch1 (does not count as st), 1dc in each st, turn.
Rows 3–25: Rep Row 2.
Fasten off.

Edging
Round 1: Using a 2.5mm (US B-1 to C-2) hook and A, with RS facing join in yarn at centre bottom of square with a sl st, 1dc in same st, *1dc in each st to corner, 3dc in corner st, 1dc in each row-end to next corner, 3dc in corner st; rep from * once more, 1dc in each st to beg of round, sl st to join.
Fasten off and sew in ends (see page 123).
Round 2: With RS facing, join B at centre bottom with a sl stBLO, *(sl stBLO, ch2, sl stBLO) in next st, sl stBLO in next st; rep from * to beg of round, sl st to join.
Fasten off and sew in ends.

CANDELABRA ARMS

Arm 1: Using a 2.5mm (US B-1 to C-2) hook and Gold, ch17.
Starting in second ch from hook, sl st in back bump of each ch to end.
Fasten off.

Arm 2: Using a 2.5mm (US B-1 to C-2) hook and Gold, ch27.
Starting in second ch from hook, sl st in back bump of each ch to end.
Fasten off.

Arm 3: Using a 2.5mm (US B-1 to C-2) hook and Gold, ch37.
Starting in second ch from hook, sl st in back bump of each ch to end.
Fasten off.

Arm 4: Using a 2.5mm (US B-1 to C-2) hook and Gold, ch47.
Starting in second ch from hook, sl st in back bump of each ch to end.
Fasten off.

STEM

Using a 2.5mm (US B-1 to C-2) hook and Gold, ch20.
Starting in second ch from hook, sl st in each ch to end.
Fasten off.

BASE

Using a 2.5mm (US B-1 to C-2) hook and Gold, ch7.
Row 1: Starting in second ch from hook, 1dc in each ch to end, turn. (*6 sts*)
Row 2: Ch1 (does not count as st), dc2tog, 1dc in each of next 2 sts, dc2tog. (*4 sts*)
Fasten off.
Using a 2mm (US steel size 4) hook, sl st around edge of base.

FINISHING

Block the square (see page 123).

Starting with the longest arm, position and pin the four arms in place, creating the curve and making sure they are evenly spaced. Stitch in place with a sewing needle and thread. Using a sewing needle and thread, stitch the base and the stem in place, using the photo as a guide.

Using a yarn needle and Golden Yellow, stitch straight stitches (see page 126) to create the nine flames. Use Gold to add a glitter thread to each flame centre.

Using Royal, decorate the square with French knots (see page 127).

hanukkah candelabra

This Christmas Wreath square is a beautifully simple make that would be perfect for Christmas cards or gift tags. It can be decorated with anything you may have to hand such as sequins, beads or even simple French knots in coloured wool or thread.

christmas wreath

SKILL RATING ● ○ ○

YARN AND MATERIALS

FOR THE BACKGROUND SQUARE:
Rowan Handknit Cotton (100% cotton), DK (light worsted) weight, 85m (92yd) per 50g (1¾oz) ball
    1 ball of Straw shade 381 (yellow) (A)
    Small amount of Rosso shade 215 (red) (B)

FOR THE WREATH:
King Cole Moments (100% polyester), DK (light worsted) weight, 90m (98yd) per 50g (1¾oz) ball
    Small amount of Emerald shade 3228 (green) (C)

Cascade 220 Superwash (100% wool), DK (light worsted) weight, 200m (218yd) per 100g (3½oz) ball
    Small amount of Peridot shade 286 (light green) (D)

Short length of narrow red ribbon

Small bells/beads/stars/sequins

Small amounts of red and white embroidery thread (floss) (optional)

HOOK AND EQUIPMENT
6mm (US J-10) crochet hook
3.5mm (US E-4) crochet hook
3mm (US D) crochet hook
Yarn needle
Blocking mat and pins
Hot glue gun

TENSION (GAUGE)
Exact tension is not important for this project.

FINISHED MEASUREMENTS
9.5 x 9.5cm (3¾ x 3¾in)

ABBREVIATIONS
See page 127.

BACKGROUND SQUARE
Using a 3.5mm (US E-4) hook and A, ch17.
Row 1: Starting in second ch from hook, 1dc in back bump of each ch to end, turn. (*16 sts*)
Row 2: Ch1 (does not count as st), 1dc in each st, turn.
Rows 3–18: Rep Row 2.
Fasten off.

Edging
Round 1: Using a 3mm (US D) hook and A, with RS facing join A at centre bottom of square with a sl st, 1dc in same st, *1dc in each st to corner, 3dc in corner st, 1dc in each row-end to next corner, 3dc in corner st; rep from * once more, 1dc in each st to beg of round, sl st to join.
Fasten off and sew in ends (see page 123).
Round 2: With RS facing, join B at centre bottom with a sl stBLO, [ch1, sl stBLO in next st] to beg of round, sl st to join.
Fasten off and sew in ends.

WREATH
Using a 6mm (US J-10) hook and 2 strands of C and 2 strands of D held together, ch23.
Round 1: Starting in second ch from hook, sl st in back bump of each ch to end, sl st in first st to join into a ring. (*22 sts*)
Fasten off and sew in ends.
Trim wreath if needed to neaten it.

FINISHING
Block the square (see page 123).
    Decorate the wreath with small bells/beads/stars/sequins by either stitching or gluing them into place. Stick the wreath to the square using a hot glue gun. Tie the ribbon into a small bow and attach to the top of the wreath.
    Optional: Two candy canes can be stitched at the top corners of the square using small amounts of red and white embroidery thread (floss).

A Christmas tree that is small enough to fit on anyone's mantlepiece and can be decorated as much as or little as you want. The glittery yarn used to create the boughs adds a festive twinkle, and with snow and glitter added around the base of the tree trunk your Christmas scene is complete.

christmas tree

SKILL RATING ● ● ○

YARN AND MATERIALS

FOR THE BACKGROUND SQUARE:
Rowan Handknit Cotton (100% cotton), DK (light worsted) weight, 85m (92yd) per 50g (1¾oz) ball
  1 ball of Straw shade 381 (yellow) (A)
  Small amount of Rosso shade 215 (red) (B)

FOR THE DECORATION:
Cascade Heritage (75% wool, 25% nylon), 4-ply (fingering) weight, 400m (437yd) per 100g (3½oz) skein (hank)
  Small amounts of:
  Sage shade 5635 (soft green) (C)
  Herb shade 5658 (green) (D)
  White shade 5682 (E)

Anchor Artiste Metallic (20% polyester, 80% viscose), 4-ply (fingering) weight, 100m (109yd) per 25g (⅞oz) ball
  Small amount of Green shade 322 (F)

Small beads/stars/sequins
Short twig for trunk of tree
Glitter glue (optional)

HOOK AND EQUIPMENT
3.5mm (US E-4) crochet hook
3mm (US-D) crochet hook
2mm (US steel size 4) crochet hook
Yarn needle
Blocking mat and pins
Hot glue gun

TENSION (GAUGE)
Exact tension is not important for this project.

FINISHED MEASUREMENTS
9.5 x 9.5cm (3¾ x 3¾in)

ABBREVIATIONS
See page 127.

BACKGROUND SQUARE
Using a 3.5mm (US E-4) hook and A, ch17.
Row 1: Starting in second ch from hook, 1dc in back bump of each ch to end, turn. (*16 sts*)
Row 2: Ch1 (does not count as st), 1dc in each st, turn.
Rows 3–18: Rep Row 2.
Fasten off.

Edging
Round 1: Using a 3mm (US D) hook and A, with RS facing join in yarn at centre bottom of square with a sl st, 1dc in same st, *1dc in each st to corner, 3dc in corner st, 1dc in each row-end to next corner, 3dc in corner st; rep from * once more, 1dc in each st to beg of round, sl st to join.
Fasten off and sew in ends (see page 123).
Round 2: With RS facing, join B at centre bottom with a sl stBLO, [ch1, sl stBLO in next st] to beg of round, sl st to join.
Fasten off and sew in ends.

TREE
Using a 3mm (US D) hook and 1 strand of C and 1 strand of D held together, make a magic ring.
Round 1: 4dc into ring. (*4 sts*)
Beg working in BLO.
Round 2: [2dc in next st, 1dc in next st] twice. (*6 sts*)
Round 3: [2dc in next st, 1dc in each of next 2 sts] twice. (*8 sts*)
Round 4: [2dc in next st, 1dc in each of next 3 sts] twice. (*10 sts*)
Round 5: [2dc in next st, 1dc in each of next 4 sts] twice. (*12 sts*)
Round 6: [2dc in next st, 1dc in each of next 5 sts] twice. (*14 sts*)
Round 7: [2dc in next st, 1dc in each of next 6 sts] twice. (*16 sts*)
Round 8: [2dc in next st, 1dc in each of next 7 sts] twice. (*18 sts*)
Round 9: [2dc in next st, 1dc in each of next 8 sts] twice. (*20 sts*)
Round 10: [2dc in next st, 1dc in each of next 9 sts] twice. (*22 sts*)
Round 11: [2dc in next st, 1dc in each of next 10 sts] twice. (*24 sts*)
Round 12: [2dc in next st, 1dc in each of next 11 sts] twice. (*26 sts*)
Round 13: [2dc in next st, 1dc in each of next 12 sts] twice. (*28 sts*)

Round 14: [1dc in each of next 6 sts, 2dc in next st] 4 times. (*32 sts*)

Round 15: [1dc in each of next 7 sts, 2dc in next st] 4 times, sl st to join. (*36 sts*)
Fasten off.

Fold tree flat and push out so that front has a good curve. The flat back will be the part of the tree that is attached to the square.

From now on work only on curved front part of tree (approx. two thirds of total tree circumference), working from right to left on each row.

Row 16: Using a 2mm (US steel size 4) hook, join F in front loop of Round 15, (2htrFLO, 1dcFLO) in each st around two thirds of tree.
Fasten off.

Row 17: Missing Round 14, join F in front loop of Round 13, (2htrFLO, 1dcFLO) in each st around two thirds of tree.
Fasten off.

Row 18: Missing Round 12, join F in front loop of Round 11, (2htrFLO, 1dcFLO) in each st around two thirds of tree.
Fasten off.

Row 19: Missing Round 10, join F in front loop of Round 9, (2htrFLO, 1dcFLO) in each st around two thirds of tree.
Fasten off.

Row 20: Missing Round 8, join F in front loop of Round 7, (2htrFLO, 1dcFLO) in each st around two thirds of tree.
Fasten off.

Row 21: Missing Round 6, join F in front loop of Round 5, (2htrFLO, 1dcFLO) in each st around two thirds of tree.
Fasten off.

Row 22: Missing Round 4, join F in front loop of Round 3, (2htrFLO, 1dcFLO) in each st around two thirds of tree.
Fasten off.

Row 23: Missing Round 2, join F in front loop of Round 1, 1htrFLO in each st around two thirds of tree.
Fasten off.

Row 24: Join F in st at top of tree, (1dc, 1htr, 1dc) in same st.
Fasten off.
Thread yarn ends through to inside or back of tree.

FINISHING

Block the square (see page 123).

Decorate the tree with small beads/stars/sequins, either stitching or gluing them in place.

Stick or sew the tree to the square using a needle and thread or hot glue gun. Glue the twig into the base of the tree for the trunk.

Using E work some small French knots (see page 127) on the square for snow, with some across the bottom of the square under the tree.

Add a little glitter glue if desired (optional).

A bright red letter box, a pile of presents and snow – a square to get you in the mood for all things Christmas! Whether made as one square for some Christmas bunting, a gift tag or a Christmas card, this little festive crochet square is very quick and simple to make.

christmas letter box and presents

SKILL RATING ● ○ ○

YARN AND MATERIALS
FOR THE BACKGROUND SQUARE:
Rowan Summerlite 4 ply (100% cotton), 4-ply (fingering) weight, 175m (191yd) per 50g (1¾oz) ball
- 1 ball of Aqua shade 433 (turquoise) (A)

Cascade Ultra Pima (100% cotton), DK (light worsted) weight, 200m (220yd) per 100g (3½oz) skein (hank)
- Small amount of Tomato shade 3823 (red) (B)

FOR THE LETTER BOX AND PRESENTS:
Cascade Heritage (75% wool, 25% nylon), 4-ply (fingering) weight, 400m (437yd) per 100g (3½oz) skein (hank)
- Small amounts of:
  Forged Iron shade 5736 (dark grey)
  Red shade 5607
  Limestone shade 5681 (beige)
  White shade 5682

Anchor Artiste Metallic (20% polyester, 80% viscose), 4-ply (fingering) weight, 100m (109yd) per 25g (⅞oz) ball
- Small amount of Gold shade 300

Small piece of cardboard

HOOK AND EQUIPMENT
3mm (US D) crochet hook
2.5mm (US B-1 to C-2) crochet hook
2mm (US steel size 4) crochet hook
Yarn needle
Blocking pins and mat
Sewing needle and thread
Scissors for cardboard

TENSION (GAUGE)
Exact tension is not important for this project.

FINISHED MEASUREMENTS
10 x 10cm (4 x 4in)

ABBREVIATIONS
See page 127.

BACKGROUND SQUARE
Using a 3mm (US D) hook and A, ch23.
Row 1: Starting in second ch from hook, 1dc in back bump of each ch to end, turn. (*22 sts*)
Row 2: Ch1 (does not count as st), 1dc in each st, turn.
Rows 3–22: Rep Row 2.
Fasten off.

Edging
Round 1: Using a 2.5mm (US B-1 to C-2) hook and A, with RS facing join in yarn at centre bottom of square with a sl st, 1dc in same st, *1dc in each st to corner, 3dc in corner st, 1dc in each row-end to next corner, 3dc in corner st; rep from * once more, 1dc in each st to beg of round, sl st to join.
Fasten off and sew in ends (see page 123).
Round 2: With RS facing, join B at centre bottom with a sl stBLO, *sl stBLO in each of next 2 sts, ch3; rep from * to beg of round, sl st to join.
Fasten off and sew in ends.

LETTER BOX
Using a 2.5mm (US B-1 to C-2) hook and Forged Iron, ch12.
Row 1: Starting in second ch from hook, 1dc in back bump of each ch to end, turn. (*11 sts*)
Rows 2 and 3: Ch1 (does not count as st throughout), 1dc in each st, turn.
Row 4: Ch1, dc2tog, 1dc in each of next 7 sts, dc2tog, turn. (*9 sts*)
Fasten off.
Row 5: Join Red at beg of Row 4 with a sl stBLO, 1dcBLO in same st, 1dcBLO in each st, turn. (*9 sts*)
Rows 6–17: Ch1, 1dc in each st, turn.
Row 18: Ch3, starting in second ch from hook, 1dc in each of next 2 ch, 1dc in each of next 9 sts, turn. (*11 sts*)

Row 19: Ch3, starting in second ch from hook, 1dc in each of next 2 ch, 1dc in each of next 9 sts, leave rem sts unworked, turn.
Row 20: Ch1, dc2tog, 1dc in each of next 5 sts, dc2tog, leave rem sts unworked, turn. (*7 sts*)
Row 21: Ch1, sl st in next st, 1dc in next st, 1htr in each of next 3 sts, 1dc in next st, sl st in last st.
Fasten off.

Edging
Using 2mm (US steel size 4) hook and Red or Forged Iron as colours dictate, 1dc in each st or row-end around letter box, working 2dc in 1 st or row-end where needed to keep shape.

Base top edging
Using 2mm (US steel size 4) hook and Forged Iron, work a line of sl st surface crochet along top edge of base of letter box.
Fasten off.

Top edging
Using 2mm (US steel size 4) hook and Red, work a line of sl st surface crochet along Row 17 of letter box.
Fasten off and sew in ends.

LARGE PRESENT
Using 2mm (US steel size 4) hook and Red, ch10.
Row 1: Starting in second ch from hook, 1dc in back bump of each ch to end, turn. (*9 sts*)
Rows 2–6: Ch1 (does not count as st), 1dc in each st, turn.
Fasten off.

Edging
Round 1: Join Red in top right corner, *1dc in each st to corner, (1dc, ch2, 1dc) in corner st, 1dc in each row-end to next corner, (1dc, ch2, 1dc) in corner st; rep from * once more, sl st to join.
Fasten off and sew in ends.

SMALL PRESENT
Using 2mm (US steel size 4) hook and Limestone, ch7.
Row 1: Starting in second ch from hook, 1dc in back bump of each ch to end, turn. (*6 sts*)
Rows 2–4: Ch1 (does not count as st), 1dc in each st, turn.
Fasten off.

Edging
Round 1: Join Limestone in top right corner, *1dc in each st to corner, (1dc, ch2, 1dc) in corner st, 1dc in each row-end to next corner, (1dc, ch2, 1dc) in corner st; rep from * once more, sl st to join.
Fasten off and sew in ends.

FINISHING
Block the square (see page 123).

Thread Forged Iron into a yarn needle and stitch the opening of the letter box with long straight stitches (see page 126). Using Gold and a sewing needle stitch a crown shape on the letter box, and then work a French knot (see page 127) in Gold for the very top of the letter box. Using White in a yarn needle, sew two white squares onto the letter box following the photo as a guide.

Using Limestone in a sewing needle stitch French knots for dots on the large present. Tie a length of Limestone around the present, attaching to secure on the reverse. Tie a length of Red around the small present, attaching to secure on the reverse.

Using a sewing needle and thread stitch the outside edge of the letter box to the square, creating a 3-D effect to the letter box as you sew. Leave the bottom edge open.

Cut out a small rectangle of card the same width as the letter box, roughly shape into a curve and carefully insert this into the letter box through the opening at the base to form a solid shape.

Using a sewing needle and thread stitch the presents to the square. Using Red, tie a bow and sew to the top of the small present.

Using White in a yarn needle work French knots over the background and along the bottom of the square for snow.

chapter 4
projects

This blanket is all about colour and texture, using four different colours for the squares and two different crochet stitches. The pink squares are worked in bobblette stitch which has a small, raised bobble pattern, and the duck egg and chartreuse squares are worked with double treble and double crochet to create a soft puffed effect. The squares are joined with raised double crochet seams.

tutti-frutti blanket

SKILL RATING ● ● ○

YARN AND MATERIALS
Sirdar Country Classic DK (50% wool, 50% acrylic), DK (light worsted) weight, 125m (136yd) per 50g (1¾oz) ball
   5 balls of Rose Pink shade 855 (light pink) (A)
   6 balls of Pink shade 857 (dark pink) (B)
   5 balls of Chartreuse shade 866 (yellow) (C)
   5 balls of Duck Egg Blue shade 864 (D) (turquoise)
   6 balls of Oat Beige shade 851 (E) (beige)

HOOK AND EQUIPMENT
4mm (US G-6) crochet hook
3.5mm (US E-4) crochet hook
Safety pins
Yarn needle

TENSION (GAUGE)
21 sts x 26 rows = 10 x 10cm (4 x 4in) working double crochet using a 4mm (US G-6) crochet hook.

FINISHED MEASUREMENTS
Finished blanket when blocked:
115 x 95cm (45¼ x 37½in)

ABBREVIATIONS
See page 127.

SPECIAL ABBREVIATION
dcdc: Insert hook in stitch, pull loop back through, yarn over, ch2, yarn over and pull through 2 loops on the hook.

KEY POINTS:
For a neat bottom edge to each square see page 118 for details of working into the back bump of the starting chain.

Once each square is finished in the main colour, a double crochet border is worked around the edge in the same colour and then a second round is worked in the same way in E, ready for the joining process.

BOBBLETTE SQUARE
(make 20 in A, 20 in B)
Using either A or B and a 4mm (US G-6) hook, ch22.
Row 1: Starting in second ch from hook, 1dc in back bump of each ch to end, turn. (*21 sts*)
Row 2: Ch1 (does not count as st throughout), 1dc in first st, *1dcdc in next st, 1dc in next st; rep from * to end of row, turn.
Row 3: Ch1, 1dc in each st, turn.
Row 4: Ch1, 1dc in each of first 2 sts, *1dcdc in next st, 1dc in next st; rep from * to last st, 1dc in last st, turn.
Row 5: Ch1, 1dc in each st, turn.
Rows 6–21: Rep Rows 2–5.
Your last row will be a dc row.
Fasten off.

Edging
Round 1: With RS facing, using a 3.5mm (US E-4) hook, join A or B at centre of bottom edge with a sl st and 1dc in same st, 1dc in each st to bottom right-hand corner, 3dc in corner st, 1dc in each row end up right-hand edge of square to top right-hand corner, 3dc in corner st, 1dc in each st along top of square to top left-hand corner, 3dc in corner st, 1dc in each row end down left-hand edge of square to bottom left-hand corner, 3dc in corner st, 1dc in each st along bottom edge to beg of round, sl st to join.
Fasten off A or B.

tutti-frutti blanket

Round 2: Join E at centre of bottom edge, *1dc in each st to corner st, 3dc in corner st; rep from * three times, 1dc in each st to beg of round, sl st to join.
Fasten off and sew in ends (see page 123).

PUFFED SQUARES
(make 20 in C, 20 in D)
Using either C or D and a 4mm (US G-6) hook, ch22.
Row 1: Starting in second ch from hook, 1dc in back bump of each ch to end, turn. (*21 sts*)
Row 2: Ch1 (does not count as st throughout), *1dc in next st, 1dtr in next st; rep from * to last st, 1 dc in last st, turn.
Row 3: Ch1, 1dc in each st, turn.
Rows 4–19: Rep Rows 2 and 3.
Your last row will be a dc row.
Fasten off.

Edging
Round 1: With RS facing, using a 3.5mm (US E-4) hook, join C or D at centre of bottom edge with a sl st and 1dc in same st, 1dc in each st to bottom right-hand corner, 3dc in corner st, 1dc in each row end up right-hand edge of square to top right-hand corner, 3dc in corner st, 1dc in each st along top of square to top left-hand corner, 3dc in corner st, 1dc in each row end down left-hand edge of square to bottom left-hand corner, 3dc in corner st, 1dc in each st along bottom edge to beg of round, sl st to join.
Fasten off C or D.
Round 2: Join E at centre of bottom edge, *1dc in each st to corner, 3dc in corner st; rep from * three times, 1dc in each st to beg of round, sl st to join.
Fasten off E and sew in ends.

Joining
Lay the squares out on a flat surface in the correct colour pattern. Join together with safety pins as this allows you to pick up the whole blanket to work without losing the pattern. You will have a neater finish if you work all the seams in one direction first and then all the seams in the opposite direction.
Place two squares WS together, lining up the edge to be joined. Working in the two inside loops only, join the squares together with a double crochet seam. Continue to add the next two squares and so on until you have finished a complete length/width of the blanket.
When working the other way and joining squares across a seam, ch1 over the seam and continue on to the next square.

FINISHING
Once all the squares are joined, sew in all the ends.

BLANKET BORDER
Round 1: With RS facing, using a 3.5mm (US E-4) hook, join E at centre of bottom edge of blanket, ch1 (does not count as st), *1dc in each st to corner, 3dc in corner st; rep from * three times, 1dc in each st to beg of round, sl st to join.
Round 2: Rep Round 1.
Fasten off E.
Round 3: Join C at centre of bottom edge and rep Round 1.
Fasten off C.
Round 4: Join A at centre of bottom edge and rep Round 1.
Fasten off A.
Round 5: Join D at centre of bottom edge and rep Round 1.
Fasten off D.
Round 6: Join E at centre of bottom edge and rep Round 1, do not fasten off.
Round 7: Ch2 (does not count as st), *3trBLO in next st, 2trBLO in next st; rep from * all around, sl st to join.
Fasten off E.
Round 8: Join B at centre of bottom edge, ch1, 1dc in each st to beg of round, sl st to join.
Fasten off B.

Sew in ends and block the blanket (see page 123).

This very simple tissue box cover is made up of five squares of chunky stripes. Worked in an Aran (worsted) weight yarn it is lovely and quick to make and by using a 4mm (US G-6) crochet hook this yarn works up to give a good solid texture. The squares are sewn together and the top square is attached with a picot edge. For extra structure there is a basic cardboard frame inside so that the whole cover can just be popped over any new box of tissues.

square tissue box cover

SKILL RATING ● ● ●

YARN AND MATERIALS
Rowan Four Seasons (60% cotton, 40% acrylic), Aran (worsted) weight, 75m (82yd) per 50g (1¾oz) ball
- 2 balls of Summer shade 005 (peach) (A)
- 1 ball of Blossom shade 006 (light pink) (B)

Cotton or acrylic yarn, in a lighter weight and similar toning colour, for joining the seams

Cardboard (an old cardboard box is perfect)

HOOK AND EQUIPMENT
3.5mm (US E-4) crochet hook
4mm (US G-6) crochet hook
Yarn needle
Safety pins

TENSION (GAUGE)
18 sts x 18 rows = 10 x 10cm (4 x 4in) working double crochet using a 4mm (US G-6) crochet hook.

FINISHED MEASUREMENTS
14 x 14 x 14cm (5½ x 5½ x 5½in)

ABBREVIATIONS
See page 127.

KEY POINTS
For a neat bottom edge to each square see page 118 for details of working into the back bump of the starting chain.

Once each square is finished, a double crochet border is worked around the edge in the same colour as the starting/finishing stripe, ready for the joining process.

When joining the squares together, use a lighter weight cotton or acrylic yarn for a neater join.

SIDE SQUARES
(make 2 beg in A, 2 beg in B)
Each square is made up of 5 stripes.
Using a 4mm (US G-6) hook and either A or B, ch21.
Row 1: Starting in second ch from hook, 1dc in back bump of each ch to end, turn. (*20 sts*)
Rows 2 and 3: Ch1 (does not count as st throughout), 1dc in each st to end, turn.
Row 4: Ch1, 1dc in each st to end working last yrh of last st in second colour, turn.
Do not fasten off first colour but keep twisting in with second colour as you work your way up.
Row 5: Ch1, 1dcBLO in each st to end, turn.
Rows 6 and 7: Ch1, 1dc in each st to end, turn.
Row 8: Ch1, 1dc in each st to end working last yrh of last st in first colour, turn.
Do not fasten off second colour but keep twisting in with first colour as you work your way up.
Row 9: Ch1, 1dcBLO in each st to end, turn.
Rows 10 and 11: Ch1, 1dc in each st to end, turn.
Row 12: Ch1, 1dc in each st to end working last yrh of last st in second colour, turn.
Row 13: Ch1, 1dcBLO in each st to end, turn.
Rows 14 and 15: Ch1, 1dc in each st to end, turn.
Row 16: Ch1, 1dc in each st to end working last yrh of last st in first colour, turn.
Row 17: Ch1, 1dcBLO in each st to end, turn.
Rows 18 and 19: Ch1, 1 dc in each st to end, turn.
Row 20: Ch1, 1dc in each st to end.
Fasten off.

Edging
Round 1: With RS facing, using a 3.5mm (US E-4) hook, join A or B at centre of bottom edge with a sl st and 1 dc in same st, 1dc in each st to bottom right-hand corner, (1dc, ch2, 1dc) in corner st, 1dc in each row end up right-hand edge of square to top right-hand corner, (1dc, ch2, 1dc) in corner st, 1dc in each st along top edge to top left-hand corner, (1dc, ch2, 1dc) in corner st, 1dc in each row end down left-hand edge to bottom left-hand corner, (1dc, ch2, 1dc) in corner st, 1dc in each st along bottom edge to beg of round, sl st to join.
Fasten off.

TOP SQUARE
Working first stripe in A, work Rows 1–10 as for side square.
Row 11: Ch1, 1dc in each of next 5 sts, ch10, miss next 10 sts, 1dc in each of next 5 sts, turn.
Row 12: Ch1, 1dc in each st and ch to last st, 1dc in last st working last yrh in B, turn.
Rows 13–20: Work as for Rows 13–20 of side square.

EDGING
Round 1: With RS facing, using a 3.5mm (US E-4) hook, join A at centre of bottom edge with sl st and 1 dc in same st, 1dc in each st to bottom right-hand corner, 3dc in corner st, 1dc in each row end up right-hand edge to top right-hand corner, 3dc in corner st, 1dc in each st along top edge to top left-hand corner, 3dc in corner st, 1dc in each row end down left-hand edge to bottom left-hand corner, 3dc in corner st, 1dc in each st along bottom edge to beg of round, sl st to join.
Round 2: Ch1, *1dc in each st to corner, 3dc in corner st; rep from * three times, 1dc in each st to beg of round, sl st to join.
Fasten off.

JOINING
Lay the four side squares out on a flat surface, RS up, in a long line, making sure that the stripes alternate in colour all the way along.
Using the lighter weight yarn and a yarn needle, sew oversewn seams (see page 124) to join the squares together. Fold the rectangle in half to join the final side seam.

CARDBOARD FRAMEWORK
Lay the piece of cardboard on a flat surface and draw a rectangle 12cm (4¾in) high by 48cm (19in) long. Cut the rectangle out, then divide and mark it into four, for the four edges. Score lightly along the dividing lines and fold the rectangle to form a cube. Tape the sides to join.

Draw a square 12 x 12cm (4¾ x 4¾in) and cut out. Mark out a line in the centre, approx. 2cm (¾in) from the two side edges. Cut along this line to make an opening to pull the tissues through. Tape the top square on top of the sides.

FINISHING
Place the joined sides over the cardboard framework, making sure the joined seams all line up at the corners of the cube. Place the top square in position, lining up the A stripes so that they match the side stripes. Once you are happy with the positioning, use safety pins to join the top to the sides. Remove the cover from the cardboard framework.

Round 1: Using a 3.5mm (US E-4) hook, working from inside to outside, join A at centre point of one edge with a sl st and 1dc in same st worked in two inner loops, *ch1, sl st in front loop of dc just worked, ch1, sl st in front loop only of dc just worked, sl st in next st, 1dc in next st; rep from * to beg of round, sl st to join. Fasten off.

Optional: If needed to neaten around the top, work a round of double crochet just under the picot edging. Repeat around the bottom edge of the cover if needed.

SKILL RATING ● ● ○

YARN AND MATERIALS
Rico Essentials Merino DK (100% wool), DK (light worsted) weight, 120m (131yd) per 50g (1¾oz) ball
- 3 balls of Light Teal shade 81 (A) (light blue)
- 2 balls of Natural shade 60 (B) (white)
- 2 balls of Blue Green shade 82 (C) (dark blue)

HOOK AND EQUIPMENT
3.5mm (US E-4) crochet hook
4mm (US G-6) crochet hook
Yarn needle

TENSION (GAUGE)
22 sts x 28 rows = 10 x 10cm (4 x 4in) working double crochet using a 3.5mm (US E-4) crochet hook.
28 sts x 28 rows = 10 x 10cm (4 x 4in) working checks pattern using a 4mm (US G-6) crochet hook.

FINISHED MEASUREMENTS
Finished blanket when blocked:
55 x 40cm (21¾ x 15¾in)

ABBREVIATIONS
See page 127.

KEY POINTS
The checks are made by working with two colours on each row. The yarn colour for the first square will be your working yarn and the yarn for the second colour square is laid along the top of the last row, working it in as you move along the row and then brought up as needed when the squares change colour.

When changing to the second colour, work the final yarn round hook of the first coloured square in the second colour and place the first colour yarn along the top of the work as before.

Each 'stripe' is made up of four rows and each square is worked across four stitches.

For a neat bottom edge see page 118 for details of working into the back bump of the starting chain.

Baby blankets are one of my favourite things to make as they are not too big, simple in design and require a relatively small amount of yarn. With its checked pattern, and crocheted in colours to suit, this gingham blanket makes for a beautiful, handmade personal gift.

gingham baby blanket

BLANKET
Using a 3.5mm (US E-4) hook and A, ch101.
Row 1: Starting in second ch from hook, 1dc in back bump of each ch to end, turn. (*100 sts*)
Row 2: Ch1 (does not count as st throughout), 1dc in each st to end, turn.
Row 3: Change to a 4mm (US G-6) hook, join in C and ch1, lay A along top of last worked row and work over it along row, using C, 1dc in each of next 4 sts working last yrh in A, lay C along top of last row worked, using A, 1dc in each of next 4 sts working last yrh in C, lay A along top of last row worked, cont as set to end of row working 4dc in alternating colours, turn. You will have 25 squares across the row.
Rows 4–6: Rep Row 3.
At end of Row 6 fasten off C, turn.
Row 7: Using A as first yarn colour, ch1 in A, lay B along top of last worked row and work over it along row, using A, 1 dc in each of next 4 sts working last yrh in B, lay A along top of last row worked, using B, 1 dc in each of next 4 sts working last yrh in A, lay B along top of last row worked, cont as set to end of row working 4dc in alternating colours, turn.
Rows 8–10: Rep Row 7.
At end of Row 10 fasten off B, turn.
Rep Rows 3–10 until you have worked 33 different 'stripes', ending with Row 6.
Fasten off C.
Change to a 3.5mm (US E-4) hook, using A, work 2 rows of dc.
Fasten off A.

Edging
Round 1: With RS facing, using a 3.5mm (US E-4) hook, join A at centre of bottom edge with a sl st and 1dc in same st, 1dc in each st to bottom right-hand corner, 2dc in corner st, working up right-hand edge, *1dc in next row end, miss 1 row end, 2dc in next row end; rep from * to top right-hand corner, 2dc in corner st, 1dc in each st along top edge to corner, 2dc in corner st, **1dc in first row end, miss 1 row end, 2dc in next row end; rep from ** to bottom left-hand corner, 2dc in corner st, 1dc in each st along bottom edge to beg of round, sl st to join.
Fasten off.

Border
Round 1: Using a 3.5mm (US E-4) hook, join C at centre of bottom edge with a sl st and 1dc in same st, *1dc in each st to corner, 3dc in corner st; rep from * 3 times, 1dc in each st to beg of round, sl st to join.
Round 2: Rep Round 1.
Fasten off C.

Round 3: Using B, rep Round 1 working in back loops only.
Round 4: For picot edge, ch1, *1dc in each of next 2 sts, ch2; rep from * to end, sl st in beg of round to join.
Fasten off.

FINISHING
Sew in all the ends of the finished blanket (see page 123).
To get the best finish to your work, block the blanket (see page 123).

Worked in a chunky wool-blend yarn, these two cushions are all about shape and texture. To add a twist to the crochet squares used to make the cover, the four squares are stitched together in an envelope style, with the joining seam being worked in a zigzag pattern for extra detail. The cover is reversible, with one side making a feature of the joining seam, the other being finished with a large bow. The cushion pad is inserted into a square opening on the bow side, where the seams are not fully closed. These cushions can either be worked as a matching pair or in co-ordinating colours.

chunky bobbly cushions

SKILL RATING ● ● ○

YARN AND MATERIALS
Lion Brand Hue + Me (80% acrylic, 20% wool) chunky (bulky) weight, 125m (137yd) per 125g (4 ⅜oz) ball
    5 balls of Bellini shade 102 (peach) (A)
    3 balls of Desert shade 99 (light pink) (B)

35 x 35cm (14 x 14in) cushion pad
30 x 30cm (12 x 12in) cushion pad
Approx. 100cm (39½in) of co-ordinating ribbon for each cushion

HOOK AND EQUIPMENT
6.5mm (US K-10½) crochet hook
Yarn needle

TENSION (GAUGE)
13 sts x 16 rows = 10 x 10cm (4 x 4in) working double crochet using a 6.5mm (US K-10½) crochet hook.

FINISHED MEASUREMENTS
Large cushion: 42 x 42cm (16½ x 16½in)
Small cushion: 33 x 33cm (13 x 13in)

ABBREVIATIONS
See page 127.

SPECIAL ABBREVIATION
MB (make bobble large cushion): [Yrh, insert hook in st, yrh, pull hook back through work, yrh, pull through first 2 loops on hook] 5 times all in same st, yrh, pull through all loops on hook
MB (make bobble small cushion): [Yrh, insert hook in st, yrh, pull hook back through work, yrh, pull through first 2 loops on hook] 4 times all in same st, yrh, pull through all loops on hook

KEY POINTS
Once each square is finished, a double crochet border is worked around the edge in the same colour ready for the joining process.

For a neat bottom edge to each square see page 118 for details of working into the back bump of the starting chain.

LARGE CUSHION SQUARES
(make 4)
Using A, ch32.
Row 1 (WS): Starting in second ch from hook, 1dc in back bump of each ch to end, turn. (*31 sts*)
Row 2 (RS) (Bobble Row 1): Ch1 (does not count as st throughout), 1dc in each of first 3 sts, *MB in next st, 1dc in each of next 3 sts; rep from * to end of row, turn.
Row 3: Ch1, 1dc in each st to end, turn.
Row 4 (Bobble Row 2): Ch1, 1dc in first st, *MB in next st, 1dc in each of next 3 sts; rep from * to last 2 sts, MB in next st, 1dc in last st, turn.
Row 5: Ch1, 1dc in each st to end, turn.
Rep Rows 2–5 until you have 15 bobble rows in total, ending with Row 3. Your last row will be a dc row.
Fasten off.

Edging
Round 1: With RS facing, join A in centre of bottom edge with a sl st and 1dc in same st, 1dc in each st to bottom right-hand corner, 3dc in corner st, 1dc in each row end up right-hand edge of square to top right-hand corner, 3dc in corner st, 1dc in each st along top of square to top left-hand corner, 3dc in corner st, 1dc in each row end down left-hand edge of square to bottom left-hand corner, 3dc in corner st, 1dc in each st along bottom edge to beg of round, sl st to join.
Fasten off and sew in ends (see page 123).

SMALL CUSHION SQUARES
(make 4)
Using B, ch24.
Row 1 (WS): Starting in second ch from hook, 1dc in back bump of each ch to end, turn. (*23 sts*)

Row 2 (RS) (Bobble Row 1): Ch1 (does not count as st throughout), 1dc in each of first 3 sts, *MB in next st, 1dc in each of next 3 sts; rep from * to end of row, turn.
Row 3: Ch1, 1dc in each st to end, turn.
Row 4 (Bobble Row 2): Ch1, 1dc in first st, *MB in next st, 1dc in each of next 3 sts; rep from * to last 2 sts, MB in next st, 1dc in last st, turn.
Row 5: Ch1, 1dc in each st to end, turn.
Rep Rows 2–5 until you have 11 bobble rows in total, ending with Row 3. Your last row will be a dc row. Fasten off and sew in ends.

Edging
Round 1: With RS facing, join B in centre of bottom edge with a sl st and 1dc in same st, 1dc in each st to bottom right-hand corner, 3dc in corner st, 1dc in each row end up right-hand edge of square to top right-hand corner, 3dc in corner st, 1dc in each st along top of square to top left-hand corner, 3dc in corner st, 1dc in each row end down left-hand edge of square to bottom left-hand corner, 3dc in corner st, 1dc in each st along bottom edge to beg of round, sl st to join. Fasten off and sew in ends.

JOINING
Lay the four squares out on a flat surface, RS facing up, to make one large square. Starting at the bottom of the vertical centre seam, join A with 1dc. With yarn coming up from underneath, work sl st from side to side to join the squares together (see page 124). It is helpful to keep your work flat on a table as you join the seams so that you are looking down on to your work.

At the end of the vertical seam leave approx. 200cm (79in) long yarn tail and fasten off. Sew in ends. Join the horizontal seam in the same way, again leaving a long yarn tail when you fasten off.

Now turn the large square of four joined pieces over. Fold each of the squares in half diagonally so that you have four triangles. Pick up one of the long yarn ends and continue working the zigzag sl st join until approx. 8cm (3¼in) from the centre of the cushion cover where all the points meet. Rep with the other long yarn tail. For the two seams where there is no yarn tail, join in the yarn where the seam ends and finish joining the seam as above. By finishing the seams a little before the centre point you have created the opening for the cushion pad to be inserted.

Fasten off and sew in ends.

FINISHING
Insert the cushion pad. Thread the ribbon from the front through to the back into the tips of the top and bottom triangles, then from the back through to the front, into the two tips of the side triangles. Your ribbon will now be in the right position for you to close the hole at the back of the cover and tie a large bow.

This bag certainly delivers on the fun – fun to make, fun to look at and fun to use! Made of two large squares for the front and back and three small squares at each side, it couldn't be simpler in design and with the added bobbles and finishing ribbon you can bring in whatever colour scheme you choose.

bobbly grab bag

SKILL RATING ● ● ○

YARN AND MATERIALS
Rico Essentials Soft Merino (100% wool), Aran (worsted) weight, 100m (109yd) per 50g (1¾oz) ball
  6 balls of Beige shade 081 (A)

Rico Essentials Merino DK (100% wool), DK (light worsted) weight, 120m (131yd) per 50g (1¾oz) ball
  1 ball of Patina shade 35 (turquoise blue) (B)
  1 ball of Natural shade 60 (white) (C)
  1 ball of Orchid shade 07 (pink) (D)
  1 ball of Mustard shade 70 (yellow) (E)

Approx. 32 x 10cm (12½ x 4in) of cardboard to line base of bag

Pair of bag handles

75cm (29½in) of co-ordinating ribbon

HOOK AND EQUIPMENT
3.5mm (US E-4) crochet hook
4mm (US G-6) crochet hook.
Yarn needle

TENSION (GAUGE)
20 sts x 24 rows = 10 x 10cm (4 x 4in) working double crochet using a 4mm (US G-6) crochet hook and Rico Essentials Soft Merino Aran.

FINISHED MEASUREMENTS
32 x 32 x 10cm (12½ x 12½ x 4in)

ABBREVIATIONS
See page 127.

SPECIAL ABBREVIATION
MB (make bobble): Using colour as noted in pattern, 6tr in same st, leaving last loop of each st on hook, yrh using A, and pull through all loops on hook

KEY POINTS
For a neat bottom edge to each square see page 118 for details of working into the back bump of the starting chain.

Once each square is finished in the main colour, a double crochet border is worked around the edge in the same colour, ready for the joining process.

FRONT AND BACK SQUARES
(make 2)
Using a 4mm (US G-6) hook and A, ch64.
Row 1 (RS): Starting in second ch from hook, 1dc in back bump of each ch to end, turn. (*63 sts*)
Rows 2–6: Ch1 (does not count as st throughout), 1dc in each st to end, turn.
**Row 7 (Bobble Row 1): Lay D and E along top of last row, using A, ch1, 1dc in each of next 7 sts making sure that D and E are worked in along row, *bring up D, MB in next st using D, using A, 1dc in each of next 7 sts making sure that D and E are worked in along row, bring up E, MB in next st using E, using A, 1dc in each of next 7 sts; rep from * to end of row, turn.
Rows 8–13: Ch1, 1dc in each st to end, turn.
Row 14 (Bobble Row 2): Lay B and C along top of last row, using A, 1dc in each of next 3 sts making sure that B and C are worked in along row, *bring up B, MB in next st using B, using A, 1dc in each of next 7 sts making sure that B and C are worked in along row, bring up C, MB in next st using C, using A, 1dc in each of next 7 sts; rep from * to end of row ending final rep with 1dc in each of last 3 sts, turn.
Rows 15–20: Ch1, 1dc in each st to end, turn.
Rep from ** until you have worked 8 bobble rows in total, ending with Row 14.
Next 7 rows: Using A, ch1, 1dc in each st to end, turn.
Fasten off.

Edging
Round 1: With RS facing, using a 3.5mm (US E-4) hook, join A at centre of bottom edge with a sl st and 1dc in same st, 1dc in each st to bottom right-hand corner, 3dc in corner st, 1dc in each row end up right-hand edge to top right-hand corner, 3dc in corner st, 1dc in each st along top edge to top left-hand corner, 3dc in corner st, 1dc in each row end down left-hand edge to bottom left-hand corner, 3dc in corner st, 1dc in each st along bottom edge to beg of round, sl st to join. Fasten off and sew in ends (see page 123).

SIDE SQUARES
(make 6)
Using a 4mm (US G-6) hook and A, ch20.
Row 1: Starting in second ch from hook, 1dc in back bump of each ch to end, turn. (*19 sts*)
Rows 2-6: Ch1 (does not count as st throughout), 1dc in each st to end, turn.
Row 7 (Bobble Row 1): Lay B and C along top of last row, using A, ch1, 1dc in each of next 5 sts making sure that B and C are worked in along row, bring up B, MB in next st using B, using A, 1dc in each of next 7 sts making sure that B and C are worked in along row, bring up C, MB in next st in C, using A, 1dc in each of next 5 sts, turn.
Rows 8-14: Ch1, 1dc in each st to end, turn.
Row 15 (Bobble Row 2): Lay D and E along top of last row, using A, 1dc in each of next 5 sts making sure D and E are worked in along row, bring up D, MB in next st in D, using A, 1dc in each of next 7 sts making sure that D and E are worked in along row, bring up E, MB in next st in E, using A, 1dc in each of next 5 sts, turn.
Rows 16-22: Ch1, 1dc in each st to end, turn.
Fasten off.

Edging
Round 1: With RS facing, using a 3.5mm (US E-4) hook, join A at centre of bottom edge with a sl st and 1dc in same st, 1dc in each st to bottom right-hand corner, 3dc in corner st, 1dc in each row end up right-hand edge to top right-hand corner, 3dc in corner st, 1dc in each st along top edge to top left-hand corner, 3dc in corner st, 1dc in each row end down left-hand edge to bottom left-hand corner, 3dc in corner st, 1dc in each st along bottom edge to beg of round, sl st to join. Fasten off and sew in ends.

BASE
Using a 3.5mm (US E-4) hook and A, ch64.
Row 1: Starting in second ch from hook, 1dc in back bump of each ch to end, turn. (*63 sts*)
Rows 2-23: Ch1 (does not count as st throughout), 1dc in each st to end, turn.
Do not turn or fasten off at end of Row 23, work 2 more dc in last st, 1dc in each row end down left-hand edge to last st, 3dc in last st, 1dc in each st along bottom edge to last st, 3dc in last st, 1dc in each row end up right-hand side to last st, 3dc in last st, 1dc in each st along top edge, sl st in beg of round to join.
Fasten off and sew in ends.

JOINING
Lay three of the side squares in a vertical row and join the two touching seams with a sl st seam (see page 124) in the two inside loops. You will now have a panel of three side squares. Repeat with the other three side squares.

Join the two side panels to the short edges of the base panel in the same way. You now have a long strip that will run down the side, along the base and up the other side of the bag.

Pin the front and back squares to the side and base piece. Join the seams with a sl st seam in the two inside loops of the edges. Fasten off and sew in ends.

Edging
Using a 4mm (US G-6) hook, join B at any point around top edge with a sl st and 1dc in same st, 1dc in each st all around top of bag, sl st in beg of round to join. Do not fasten off.

The ruffle is a double ruffle with one worked in the front loop only of the last round and the second in the back loop only of the last round.
Ruffle 1: Change to a 3.5mm (US E-4) hook, ch3 (does not count as st throughout), *3trFLO in next st, 2trFLO in following st; rep from * all around top of bag, sl st in beg of round to join.
Ruffle 2: Ch3, *3trBLO in next st, 2trBLO in following st; rep from * all around top of bag, sl st in beg of round to join.
Fasten off and sew in ends.

FINISHING
Position the handles and stitch securely in place.

Cut a piece of cardboard to the shape of the base and place inside the bottom for extra strength.

Tie the ribbon around one of the handles.

For a contemporary look to your dining table these chequered place mats and coasters will fit the bill with their striking appearance. Crocheted in an Aran (worsted) weight cotton yarn with a smaller sized crochet hook, they work up to give a firm texture.

chequered place mats and coasters

SKILL RATING ● ● ○

YARN AND MATERIALS
Wool and the Gang Shiny Happy Cotton (100% cotton), Aran (worsted) weight, 142m (155yd) per 100g (3½oz) ball
  1 ball of Timber Wolf (light brown) (A)
  1 ball of Ivory White (B)

HOOK AND EQUIPMENT
3.5mm (US E-4) crochet hook
4mm (US G-6) crochet hook
Yarn needle

TENSION (GAUGE)
19 sts x 22 rows = 10 x 10cm (4 x 4in) working double crochet using a 4mm (US G-6) crochet hook.
20 sts x 20 rows = 10 x 10cm (4 x 4in) working chequered pattern using a 4mm (US G-6) crochet hook.

FINISHED MEASUREMENTS
Finished mats after blocking:
Place mats: 22 x 22cm (8¾ x 8¾in)
Coasters: 10 x 10cm (4 x 4in)

ABBREVIATIONS
See page 127.

KEY POINTS
The checks are made by working with two colours on each row. The yarn colour for the first square will be your working yarn and the yarn for the second colour square is laid along the top of the last row, working it in as you move along the row and then brought up as needed when the squares change colour.

When changing to the second colour, work the final yarn round hook of the first colour square in the second colour and place the first colour yarn along the top of the work to work in as you move along the row.

Each 'stripe' in the place mat is made up of six rows and each square is worked across six stitches. On the coasters, each 'stripe' is made up of four rows and each square is worked across four stitches.

For a neat bottom edge see page 118 for details of working into the back bump of the starting chain.

PLACE MATS
(make 2)
Using a 4mm (US G-6) hook and A, ch43.
Row 1: Lay B along top of chain, starting in second ch from hook, working either in each ch or back bump of ch, using A, 1dc in each of next 6 ch working last yrh in B, lay A along top of chain, using B, 1dc in each of next 6 ch working last yrh in A, cont as set to end of row working 6dc in alternating colours, turn. (42 sts)
Row 2: Ch1 (does not count as st throughout), lay B along top of row, using A, 1dc in each of next 6 sts working last yrh in B, lay A along top of row, using B, 1dc in each of next 6 sts working last yrh in A, cont as set to end of row working 6dc in alternating colours, turn.
Rows 3–6: Rep Row 2, working last yrh of final row in B, turn.
Row 7: Using B, ch1, lay A along top of row, 1dc in each of next 6 sts working last yrh in A, lay B along top of row, using A, 1dc in each of next 6 sts working last yrh in B, cont as set to end of row working 6dc in alternating colours, turn.
Rows 8–12: Rep Row 7, working last yrh of final row in A, turn.
Row 13: Rep Row 2.
Rep Rows 2–13, then rep Rows 2–12.
Fasten off.

Edging
Round 1: With RS facing, using a 3.5mm (US E-4) hook, join A at centre of bottom edge with a sl st and 1 dc in same st, 1dc in each st to bottom right-hand corner, (1dc, ch2, 1dc) in corner st, 1dc in each row end up right-hand edge of square to top right-hand corner, (1dc, ch2, 1dc) in corner st, 1dc in each st along top edge to top left-hand corner, (1dc, ch2, 1dc) in corner st, 1dc in each row end down left-hand edge to bottom left-hand corner, (1dc, ch2, 1dc) in corner st, 1dc in each st along bottom edge to beg of round, sl st to join.
Round 2: Ch1, *1dcBLO in each st to corner, (1dc, ch2, 1dc) in corner; rep from * three times, 1dcBLO in each st to beg of round, sl st to join.
Fasten off and sew in ends (see page 123).

COASTERS
(make 2)
Using a 3.5mm (US E-4) hook and A, ch17.
Row 1: Lay B along top of chain, starting in second ch from hook, working either in each ch or back bump of ch, using A, 1dc in each of next 4 ch working last yrh in B, lay A along top of chain, using B, 1dc in each of next 4 ch working last yrh in A, cont as set to end of row working 4dc in alternating colours, turn. (*16 sts*)
Row 2: Ch1 (does not count as st throughout), lay B along top of row, using A, 1dc in each of next 4 sts working last yrh in B, lay A along top of row, using B, 1dc in each of next 4 sts working last yrh in A, cont as set to end of row working 4dc in alternating colours, turn.
Rows 3 and 4: Rep Row 2, working last yrh of final row in B, turn.
Row 5: Using B, ch1, lay A along top of row, 1dc in each of next 4 sts working last yrh in A, lay B along top of row, using A, 1dc in each of next 4 sts working last yrh in B, cont as set to end of row working 4dc in alternating colours, turn.
Rows 6-8: Rep Row 5, working last yrh of final row in A, turn.
Row 9: Rep Row 2.
Rep Rows 2-9, then rep Rows 2-8.
Fasten off.

Edging
Round 1: With RS facing, using a 3.5mm (US E-4) hook, join A at centre of bottom edge with a sl st and 1 dc in same st, 1dc in each st to bottom right-hand corner, (1dc, ch2, 1dc) in corner st, 1dc in each row end up right-hand edge of square to top right-hand corner, (1dc, ch2, 1dc) in corner st, 1dc in each st along top edge to top left-hand corner, (1dc, ch2, 1dc) in corner st, 1dc in each row end down left-hand edge to bottom left-hand corner, (1dc, ch2, 1dc) in corner st, 1dc in each st along bottom edge to beg of round, sl st to join.
Round 2: Ch1, *1dcBLO in each st to corner, (1dc, ch2, 1dc) in corner; rep from * three times, 1dcBLO in each st to beg of round, sl st to join.
Fasten off and sew in ends.

FINISHING
The mats and coasters will benefit hugely from blocking (see page 123) to give a crisp, neat finish.

daisy-and-dot hot water bottle cover

Nothing shouts cosy more than a crocheted hot water bottle cover and it makes a perfect handmade gift. Worked in rich autumnal colours, this design brings a little touch of luxury to those chilly nights. The squares are worked in the round with either a dot or daisy stitched onto the completed square, then joined on the reverse to give a flat finish to the cover. A beautiful bobbly border adds the finishing touch. The cover opens at the top with a drawstring to close around the neck of the hot water bottle. Worked in a DK (light worsted) weight yarn it has a soft feel but a good, firm texture.

SKILL RATING ● ● ●

YARN AND MATERIALS
Rico Essentials Merino DK (100% wool), DK (light worsted) weight, 120m (131yd) per 50g (1¾oz) ball
- 2 balls of Orchid shade 07 (dark pink) (A)
- 2 balls of Mustard shade 70 (yellow) (B)
- 2 balls of Rose shade 01 (light pink) (C)

2L (4¼ US pint) hot water bottle
Approx. 75cm (29½in) of ribbon or cord

HOOK AND EQUIPMENT
3mm (US D) crochet hook
3.5mm (US E-4) crochet hook

Stitch markers
Safety pins
Yarn needle

TENSION (GAUGE)
27 sts x 30 rows = 10 x 10cm (4 x 4in) working double crochet using a 3.5mm (US E-4) crochet hook.

FINISHED MEASUREMENTS
35 x 21cm (13¾ x 8¼in) length by width

ABBREVIATIONS
See page 127.

SPECIAL ABBREVIATION
MB: (make a bobble): [yrh, insert hook in st, yrh, pull through st as if starting htr, pull loop up to htr height] 4 times in same st, yrh, pull through all loops on hook, ch1

KEY POINTS
Once each square is finished in the main colour, a double crochet border is worked around the edge in C, ready for the joining process.

For a neat bottom edge to each square see page 118 for details of working into the back bump of the starting chain.

SQUARES
(make 12 in A, 12 in B)
Using a 3.5mm (US E-4) hook and either A or B, make a magic ring.
Round 1: 8dc into ring, sl st in first st to join. (*8 sts*)
Round 2: Ch1 (does not count as st throughout), 1dc in next st, (1dc, ch2, 1dc) in next st, PM in centre of 2-ch (first corner), 1dc in next st, (1dc, ch2, 1dc) in next st, PM in centre of 2-ch (second corner), 1dc in next st, (1dc, ch2, 1dc) in next st, PM in centre of 2-ch (third corner), 1dc in next st, (1dc, ch2, 1dc) in next st, PM in centre of 2-ch (fourth corner), sl st in beg of round to join. (*12 sts and four 2-ch sps*)
Round 3: Ch1, *1dc in each dc to marker, at marker (1dc, ch2, 1dc) in 2-ch sp, PM in centre of 2-ch; rep from * three times, 1dc in each dc to end, sl st in beg of round to join. (*20 sts and four 2-ch sps*)
Rounds 4–9: Work as for Round 3; each round will increase by 8 sts.
At end of Round 9 you will have 68 sts and four 2-ch sps.
Fasten off C or D.
Round 10: Join C at centre of bottom edge with a sl st and 1dc in same st. Work a round of dc, working (1dc, ch2, 1dc) in each corner 2-ch sp as for previous rounds. (*76 sts and four 2-ch sps*)
Fasten off and sew in ends (see page 123).

JOINING
Lay the 24 squares out on a flat surface, RS down, in the correct colour pattern. Join together with safety pins as this allows you to pick up the whole cover to work without losing the pattern. You will have a neater finish if you work all the seams in one direction first and then all the seams in the opposite direction.

Place two squares RS together, lining up the edge to be joined. Working in the two inside loops only, join the squares together with a double crochet seam (see page 124). Continue to add the next two squares and so on until you have finished a complete length/width of the cover.

When working the other way and joining squares across a seam, ch1 over the seam and continue on to the next square.

Once all of the squares are joined in one large rectangle (leaving bottom edge and one side edge open), sew in all the ends. If needed block (see page 123) the rectangle of squares at this point.

DAISIES AND DOTS

For each of the squares in B, thread a length of A in a yarn needle and oversew the central circle of the square in satin stitch (see page 127) to form a dot. Finish off on the WS and sew in ends.

For each of the squares in A, thread a length of B in a yarn needle and oversew the central circle of the square to form a dot. This will be the centre of the daisy. Fasten off on the WS. Using C and a yarn needle, work single straight stitches (see page 126) around the centre of the flower, making all the stitches roughly the same length. When the first round of petals is complete, work a second round of slightly longer stitches that are spaced a little further apart. Fasten off on the WS.

FINISHING

Fold the cover in half, RS together, and join the two side edges together with the same double crochet seam method used to join the squares. Turn the tube RS out and decide which will be the front and the back. Mark the front with a stitch marker.

TOP EDGE

Round 1: Using a 3mm (US D) hook, join C at centre back of top edge with a sl st and 1dc in same st, work dc around top edge, sl st in beg of round to join.
Round 2: Ch1, 1dc in each st around, sl st in beg of round to join.
Round 3 (eyelets for drawstring): Ch1, *4dc, 3ch, miss 3 sts; rep from * all around, working 1dc in each of any rem sts, sl st in beg of round to join.
Round 4: Ch1, 1dc in each st and ch around, sl st in beg of round to join.
Rounds 5–21: Ch1, 1dc in each st around, sl st in beg of round to join.
Fasten off C.
Round 22 (Bobble Row): Join B at centre back of top edge with a sl st, sl st in next st, MB in next st, *sl st in each of next 2 sts, MB in next st; rep from * all around, working a sl st in each of any rem sts, sl st in beg of round to join.
Fasten off.

Insert the hot water bottle at this point through the opening at the bottom of the cover.

BOTTOM EDGE

Pin bottom edge of cover to join front and back together.
Row 1: With RS facing, join C at bottom right-hand corner. Using a 3mm (US D) hook join the two edges with a double crochet seam.
Fasten off and sew in ends.
Row 2: Join B at bottom right-hand corner, *sl st in each of next 2 sts, MB in next st; rep from * to end, working a sl st in each of any rem sts.
Fasten off.
Thread the gold ribbon or cord through the eyelets and tie in a bow at the front.

This autumn garland with its seasonal motifs will certainly welcome in the cosy season wherever it is hung. It's made up of seven squares in total, each having a different autumn picture on it, with each of the items being made separately and stitched onto the crocheted square. I used a cotton DK (light worsted) weight yarn for the squares and then all the individual motifs are worked in a 4-ply (fingering) yarn to keep them small and detailed.

autumn garland

SKILL RATING ● ● ●

YARN AND MATERIALS
Cascade Ultra Pima (100% cotton), DK (light worsted) weight, 200m (220yd) per 100g (3½oz) skein (hank)

FOR THE CROCHET SQUARES:
1 skein of Natural shade 3718 (off-white) (A)
1 skein of Ginger shade 3769 (dark orange) (B)

FOR THE MOTIFS:
Autumn leaves:
　Coral shade 3752 (light orange) (F)
　Ginger shade 3769 (dark orange) (B)
　Rich Gold shade 3866 (dark yellow) (E)
Toadstool:
　Wine shade 3713 (deep red) (C)
　White shade 3728 (D)
　Rich Gold shade 3866 (dark yellow) (E)
　Summer Moss shade 3780 (green) (G)
Pumpkin:
　Coral shade 3752 (light orange) (F)
　Summer Moss shade 3780 (green) (G)
Apples:
　Wine shade 3713 (deep red) (C)
　Summer Moss shade 3780 (green) (G)
　Taupe shade 3759 (light brown) (H)
Acorns:
　Rich Gold shade 3866 (dark yellow) (E)
　Summer Moss shade 3780 (green) (G)
　Taupe shade 3759 (light brown) (H)
Oak leaves:
　Wine shade 3713 (deep red) (C)
　Rich Gold shade 3866 (dark yellow) (E)
Pointed mushroom:
　Taupe shade 3759 (light brown) (H)
　Coral shade 3752 (light orange) (F)
　Rich Gold shade 3866 (dark yellow) (E)
　Summer Moss shade 3780 (green) (G)

Approx. 1.5m (59in) of cord
Ribbon (optional)

HOOK AND EQUIPMENT
2.5mm (US B-1 to C-2) crochet hook
3.5mm (US E-4) crochet hook
Stitch marker
Yarn needle
Sewing thread and needle
Spray starch

TENSION (GAUGE)
23 sts x 26 rows = 10 x 10cm (4 x 4in) working double crochet using a 3.5mm (US E-4) crochet hook.

FINISHED MEASUREMENTS
Finished garland length = Approx. 140cm (55in)
Each finished square = 10 x 10cm (4 x 4in)

ABBREVIATIONS
See page 127.

KEY POINTS
For a neat bottom edge to each square see page 118 for details of working into the back bump of the starting chain.

SQUARES
Using a 3.5mm (US E-4) hook and A, ch20.
Row 1: Starting in second ch from hook, 1dc in back bump of each ch to end, turn. (*19 sts*)
Row 2: Ch1 (does not count as st throughout), 1dc in each st to end, turn.
Rows 3-22: Ch1, 1dc in each st to end, turn. Fasten off.

Edging
Round 1: With RS facing, join A at centre of bottom edge with a sl st and 1dc in same st, 1dc in each st to bottom right-hand corner, 3dc in corner st, 1dc in each row end up right-hand edge of square to top right-hand corner, 3dc in corner st, 1dc in each st along top of square to top left-hand corner, 3dc in corner st, 1dc in each row end down left-hand edge of square to bottom left-hand corner, 3dc in corner st, 1dc in each st along bottom edge to beg of round, sl st to join. Fasten off A.
Round 2: Join in B at centre of bottom edge with a sl stBLO and 1dcBLO in same st, *1dcBLO in each st to corner, 3dcBLO in corner st; rep from * around, 1dcBLO in each st to beg of round, sl st to join.
Round 3: Ch1, *1dc in next st, ch1 and sl st back in front loop of dc, 1dc in next st, ch1 and sl st back in front loop only of dc just worked, sl st in next st; rep from * all around.
Fasten off and sew in ends (see page 123).

AUTUMN LEAVES MOTIF
AUTUMN LEAF
(make 1 in each colour)
Using a 2.5mm (US B-1 to C-2) hook and F or B, make a magic ring.
Round 1: 5dc into ring. (*5 sts*)
Round 2: 2dc in each st, PM for beg of round. (*10 sts*)
Round 3:
Point 1: Ch3, starting in second ch from hook, sl st in next ch, 1dc in next ch, sl st in next st on Round 2.
Point 2: Ch4, starting in second ch from hook, sl st in next ch, 1dc in next ch, 1htr in next ch, sl st in next st on Round 2.
Point 3: Ch6, starting in second ch from hook, sl st in next ch, 1dc in next ch, 1htr in next ch, 1tr in next ch, 1dtr in next ch, miss 2 sts on Round 2, sl st in next st.
Point 4: Ch4, starting in second ch from hook, sl st in next ch, 1dc in next ch, 1htr in next ch, sl st in next st on Round 2.
Point 5: Ch3, starting in second ch from hook, sl st in next ch, 1dc in next ch, sl st in next st on Round 2, work 1dc in next st working last yrh in contrasting B or F to change colour, ch5, starting in second ch from hook, sl st in each ch to base of leaf, sl st in base of leaf to join.
Fasten off leaving a long tail to sew a central vein on leaf and two side veins on each side.
Fasten off and sew in ends.

AUTUMN LEAF SQUARE FINISHING
Place the autumn leaves into position on the square and sew in place. Using E, work French knots (see page 127) on the completed square.

TOADSTOOL MOTIF
TOADSTOOL TOP
Using a 2.5mm (US B-1 to C-2) hook and C, ch14.
Row 1: Starting in second ch from hook, 1dc in each ch to end, turn. (*13 sts*)
Row 2: Ch1 (does not count as st throughout), dc2tog, 1dc in each st to last 2 sts, dc2tog, turn. (*11 sts*)
Row 3: Ch1, dc2tog, 1dc in each st to last 2 sts, dc2tog, turn. (*9 sts*)
Row 4: Ch1, dc2tog, 1dc in each st to last 2 sts, dc2tog, turn. (*7 sts*)
Row 5: Ch1, dc2tog, 1dc in each st to last 2 sts, dc2tog, turn. (*5 sts*)
Row 6: Ch1, dc2tog, 1dc in each st to last 2 sts, dc2tog, turn. (*3 sts*)
Fasten off.
Join C at right-hand corner of bottom straight edge with a sl st and 1dc in same st, 1dc in each st to last st, 3dc in last st, 1dc in each row end around curved edge of toadstool to bottom right-hand corner, 2dc in last st. This round will have created a curve to the toadstool.
Fasten off and sew in ends.
Using a yarn needle and D, work French knots over toadstool.

TOADSTOOL STALK
Using a 2.5mm (US B-1 to C-2) hook and E, ch14.
Row 1: Starting in second ch from hook, 1htr in next ch, 1dc in each ch to end, turn.
Row 2: Ch1 (does not count as st throughout), 1dc in each st in last st, 1htr in last st, turn.
Row 3: Ch1, 1dc in each st to end, do not turn, work 4dc evenly along top of stalk, working down opposite side of chain, 1dc in each ch to last ch, 1htr in last st, do not turn, ch1, sl st in each row end along bottom of stalk.
Fasten off.

TOADSTOOL SQUARE FINISHING
Place the toadstool top in position on the square and sew in place, keeping the 3-D effect to the shape of the top and leaving the bottom edge open.
Position the stalk and sew in place.
Fasten off and sew in ends.
Using G and straight stitch (see page 126), sew a few strands of grass around the bottom of the toadstool.
Using H, work French knots on the completed square.

PUMPKIN MOTIF
PUMPKIN BODY
Using a 2.5mm (US B-1 to C-2) hook and F, ch13.
Row 1: Starting in second ch from hook, 1dc in each ch to end, turn. (*12 sts*)
Row 2: Ch1 (does not count as st), 1dcBLO in each st to end, turn.
Rows 3–13: Rep Row 2.
Fasten off and sew in ends.

STALK
Using a 2.5mm (US B-1 to C-2) hook and G, ch6.
Row 1: Starting in second ch from hook, sl st in each of next 2 ch, 1dc in each of last 3 ch. Fasten off.

VINE
Using a 2.5mm (US B-1 to C-2) hook and G, ch10. Fasten off.

PUMPKIN SQUARE FINISHING
Using a yarn needle and two lengths of F, run a gathering thread along the long top edge and the long bottom edge of the pumpkin body. Carefully pull up each of the two gathering threads to create a curved pumpkin shape. If needed, to create the right shape, run a gathering thread up each of the short edges and gather. Once you have the correct pumpkin shape, pin the pumpkin in the correct position on the square and, using a sewing needle and thread, sew in place, keeping the 3-D effect of the pumpkin.
Position the stalk and attach to the square with the two yarn ends. Position the vine and attach to the square with the two yarn ends. Fasten off and sew in ends.
Using H, work French knots on the completed square.

APPLES MOTIF
APPLE
(make 2 in C, 1 in G)
Using a 2.5mm (US B-1 to C-2) hook and C or G, make a magic ring.
Round 1: 4dc into ring. (*4 sts*)
Round 2: 2dc in each st, PM for beg of round. (*8 sts*)
Round 3: [1dc in next st, 2dc in next st] 4 times. (*12 sts*)
Round 4: [1dc in each of next 2 sts, 2dc in next st] 4 times. (*16 sts*)
Rounds 5 and 6: 1dc in each st.
Round 7: [1dc in each of next 6 sts, dc2tog] twice. (*14 sts*)
Round 8: [1dc in each of next 5 sts, dc2tog] twice. (*12 sts*)

Round 9: [1dc, dc2tog] 4 times. (*8 sts*)
Fasten off and sew in ends.

APPLE STALK
(make 3)
Using a 2.5mm (US B-1 to C-2) hook and H, ch4.
Row 1: Starting in second ch from hook, sl st in each ch to end. Fasten off.

APPLE SQUARE FINISHING
Gently shape the apple by pushing the back in to the centre to create a curve at the front. Place the apples in position on the square and sew in place, keeping the 3-D effect.
Position the stalk and sew in place.
On the G apple, using C sew a few straight stitches from the top to the bottom to create a two-tone effect of the apple ripening.
Using G, sew a few straight stitches to create leaves at the top of the C apples.
Using E, work French knots on the completed square.

ACORNS MOTIF
ACORN CAP
(make 2)
Using a 2.5mm (US B-1 to C-2) hook and G, make a magic ring.
Round 1: 5dc into ring. (*5 sts*)
Round 2: 2dc in each st, PM for beg of round. (*10 sts*)
Round 3: [1 dc in next st, 2dc in next st] 5 times. (*15 sts*)
Round 4: 1dc in each st, sl st in beg of round to join.
Fasten off, leaving a yarn tail and use this to sew a small loop through bottom of cap as a stalk.

ACORN TOP
(make 2)
Using a 2.5mm (US B-1 to C-2) hook and E, make a magic ring.
Round 1: 4dc into ring. (*4 sts*)
Round 2: 2dc in each st, PM for beg of round. (*8 sts*)
Round 3: [1dc in each of next 3 sts, 2dc in next st] twice. (*10 sts*)
Rounds 4–7: 1dc in each st, sl st in beg of round to join.
Fasten off.

ACORN BRANCH
(make 1)
Using a 2.5mm (US B-1 to C-2) hook and H, ch14.
Row 1: Starting in second ch from hook, 1dc in each of next 5 ch, sl st in each ch to end. Fasten off.

ACORN SQUARE FINISHING
Insert the acorn tops into the caps and sew to secure. Gently shape the acorns by pushing the back into the centre to create a curve at the front.
Place the acorns in position on the square and sew in place, keeping the 3-D effect.
Position the branch and sew in place.
Using H, work French knots on the completed square.

OAK LEAVES MOTIF
OAK LEAF
(make 1 in C, 1 in E)
Using a 2.5mm (US B-1 to C-2) hook and C or E, ch10.
Round 1: Starting in second ch from hook, 1dc in each of next 8 ch, 3dc in last ch, working down opposite side of chain, 1dc in each of next 8 ch, sl st in base of chain to join. (*19 sts*)
Round 2:
Lobe 1: 1dc in next st, (1dc, 1htr, 1tr) in next st, ch2, sl st in next st.
Lobe 2: Ch3, 1dtr in same st, (1tr, 1htr) in next st, sl st in next st.
Lobe 3: Ch2, (1htr, 1tr) in next st, 1dtr in next st, ch2, sl st in next st.
Lobe 4: 1dc in next st, (1htr, 1tr) in next st, (1htr, 1dc) in next st, sl st in next st.
Lobe 5: Sl st in next st, ch2, 2tr in next st, sl st in next st.
Lobe 6: Sl st in next st, ch3, 1dtr in next st, 1tr in next st, (sl st, 1dc, 1htr) in next st, sl st in base of leaf.
Fasten off.

Stalk
Join contrasting E or C at base of leaf, ch5. Starting in second ch from hook, sl st in each ch to base of leaf, cont with same colour, work surface crochet up centre of leaf to create central vein. Fasten off and sew in ends.
Separate off one strand of stem colour and, using a yarn needle, sew smaller veins from the centre vein out to each lobe.
Fasten off.

OAK LEAF SQUARE FINISHING
Place the oak leaves into position on the square and sew in place. Fasten off and sew in ends.
Using E, work French knots on the completed square.

POINTED MUSHROOM MOTIF
LARGE POINTED MUSHROOM
Using a 2.5mm (US B-1 to C-2) hook and F, make a magic ring.
Round 1: 5dc into ring. (*5 sts*)
Round 2: [1dc in next st, 2dc in next st] twice, 2dc in next st, PM for beg of round. (*8 sts*)
Round 3: [1dc in each of next 3 sts, 2dc in next st] twice. (*10 sts*)
Round 4: [1dc in each of next 4 sts, 2dc in next st] twice. (*12 sts*)
Round 5: [1dc in each of next 5 sts, 2dc in next st] twice. (*14 sts*)
Round 6: [1dc in each of next 6 sts, 2dc in next st] twice. (*16 sts*)
Round 7: [1dc in each of next 7 sts, 2dc in next st] twice. (*18 sts*)
Round 8: [1dc in each of next 5 sts, 2dc in next st] 3 times, sl st in beg of round to join. (*21 sts*)
Fasten off and sew in the ends.

LARGE POINTED MUSHROOM STALK
Using a 2.5mm (US B-1 to C-2) hook and one strand of H and one strand of E held tog, ch13.
Row 1: Starting in second ch from hook, sl st in each ch to end.
Fasten off.

SMALL POINTED MUSHROOM
Using a 2.5mm (US B-1 to C-2) hook and F, make a magic ring.
Round 1: 5dc into ring. (*5 sts*)
Round 2: [1dc in next st, 2dc in next st] twice, 2dc in next st, PM for beg of round. (*8 sts*)
Round 3: [1dc in each of next 3 sts, 2dc in next st] twice. (*10 sts*)
Round 4: [1dc in each of next 4 sts, 2dc in next st] twice. (*12 sts*)
Round 5: [1dc in each of next 5 sts, 2dc in next st] twice. (*14 sts*)
Round 6: [1dc in each of next 6 sts, 2dc in next st] twice, sl st in beg of round to join. (*16 sts*)
Fasten off and sew in ends.

SMALL POINTED MUSHROOM STALK
Using a 2.5mm (US B-1 to C-2) hook and one strand of H and one strand of E held tog, ch10.
Row 1: Starting in second ch from hook, sl st in each ch to end.
Fasten off.

MUSHROOM SQUARE FINISHING
Using a yarn needle and H, sew straight stitches from the tip of each mushroom to the bottom. Place the mushrooms in position on the square and sew in place, keeping the 3-D effect to the shape of the top.

Position the stalks and sew in place.

Using G, sew a few strands of grass around the bottom of the toadstool.

Using E, work French knots on the completed square.

FINISHING

Once you have completed all the squares block (see page 123) them and spray with ironing starch. This will stop them from curling.

Tie two loop knots at each end of the length of cord. Lay it out on a flat surface and position your squares along it. Sew in place with a needle and sewing thread along the top edge of each square.

Tie small lengths of co-ordinating ribbon between each square.

TIP
If the back of your bunting will be seen when hanging, stitch small squares of fabric or felt to the reverse of each square.

This picture collage of one tree as it transitions through the seasons is such a simple project to work on, but one that really gives maximum effect once framed and displayed as a set of four images. The same leaf pattern is used for all three of the trees, just worked in different colours.

seasonal tree picture

SKILL RATING ●●○

YARN AND MATERIALS

FOR THE BACKGROUND SQUARE:
Cascade Ultra Pima (100% cotton), DK (light worsted) weight, 200m (220yd) per 100g (3½oz) skein (hank)
- 1 ball of Shell shade 3854 (light pink) (A)
- 1 ball of Reed shade 3834 (pale green) (B)
- 1 ball of Maple Sugar shade 3850 (brown) (C)

FOR THE LEAVES:
Rico Ricorumi Lamé (62% polyester, 38% nylon), DK (light worsted) weight, 50m (54yd) per 10g (⅜oz) ball
- 1 ball of Silver shade 001 (D)

Cascade Heritage (75% wool, 25% nylon), 4-ply (fingering) weight, 400m (437yd) per 100g (3½oz) skein (hank)

Spring tree small amounts each of:
- Primavera shade 5659 (bright green) (E)
- Herb shade 5658 (green) (F)
- Strawberry Cream shade 5648 (pink) (G)
- White shade 5682 (H)

Summer tree small amounts each of:
- Cedar Green shade 5684 (dark green) (I)
- Herb shade 5658 (green) (F)
- Red shade 5607 (J)

Autumn tree small amounts each of:
- Blood Orange 5642 (dark orange) (K)
- Pumpkin shade 5646 (orange) (L)
- Red shade 5607 (J)
- Moss shade 5612 (deep green) (M)

Winter tree small amount of:
- White shade 5682 (H)

4 twigs

Silver glitter glue

35 x 35cm (13¾ x 13¾in) box picture frame with four apertures of 9.5cm (3¾ x 3¾in)

HOOK AND EQUIPMENT
2.5mm (US B-1 to C-2) crochet hook
3mm (US D) crochet hook
Yarn needle
Sewing needle and thread
Hot glue gun

TENSION (GAUGE)
25 sts x 28 rows = 10 x 10cm (4 x 4in) working double crochet using a 3mm (US D) crochet hook and Cascade Ultra Pima.

FINISHED MEASUREMENTS
Framed picture: 35 x 35cm (13¾ x 13¾in)
Individual squares: approx. 9.5 x 9.5cm (3¾ x 3¾in)

ABBREVIATIONS
See page 127.

KEY POINTS
For a neat bottom edge to each square see page 118 for details of working into the back bump of the starting chain.

BACKGROUND SQUARES
(make 2 in A, 2 in B)
Using a 3mm (US D) hook and A or B, ch21.
Row 1: Starting in second ch from hook, 1dc in back bump of each ch to end, turn. (*20 sts*)
Row 2: Ch1 (does not count as st), 1dc in each st to end, turn.
Rows 3–22: Rep Row 2.
Fasten off and sew in ends (see page 123).

Edging
Round 1: With RS facing, using a 2.5mm (US B-1 to C-2) hook, join A or B at centre of bottom edge with a sl st and 1dc in same st, 1dc in each st to bottom right-hand corner, 3dc in corner st, 1dc in each row end up right-hand edge to top right-hand corner, 3dc in corner st, 1dc in each st along top edge to top left-hand corner, 3dc in corner st, 1dc in each row end down left-hand edge to bottom left-hand corner, 3dc in corner st, 1dc in each st along bottom edge to beg of round, sl st to join.
Fasten off.
Round 2: Working in back loop only, join C at centre of bottom edge with a sl st, ch1, *sl stBLO in next st, ch1; rep from * all around square, sl st in beg of round to join.
Fasten off and sew in ends.

For the spring tree:
Work 6 small leaves and 6 large leaves in each of E and F.

For the summer tree:
Work 7 small leaves and 7 large leaves in each of I and F.

For the autumn tree:
Work 6 small leaves and 6 large leaves in each of K, L and J.

SMALL LEAF
Using a 2.5mm (US B-1 to C-2) hook, ch4.
Row 1: Starting in second ch from hook, sl st in next ch, 1dc in next ch, sl st in last ch.
Fasten off.

LARGE LEAF
Using a 2.5mm (US B-1 to C-2) hook, ch5.
Row 1: Starting in second ch from hook, sl st in next ch, 1dc in next ch, 1htr in next ch, 1dc in last ch.
Fasten off.

BLOSSOM
(make 18)
Using a 2.5mm (US B-1 to C-2) hook and H, ch2.
Row 1: (Sl st, ch1, sl st, ch1, sl st) in second ch from hook.
Fasten off.

SNOW
Using a 2.5mm (US B-1 to C-2) hook and H, ch25.
Row 1: Starting in second ch from hook, 1dc in each ch to end, turn. (*24 sts*)
Row 2: Ch1 (does not count as st throughout), 1dc in each st to end, turn.
Row 3: Ch1, 1dc in each of next 5 sts, 1htr in each of next 4 sts, 1dc in each of next 9 sts, 1htr in each of next 4 sts, 1dc in each of next 2 sts, turn.
Row 4: Rep Row 3.
Fasten off, leaving a long yarn tail.

FINISHING
For the spring tree:
Using a hot glue gun stick the tree stem in the centre of one of the B squares. Making sure to spread out the different sizes and different colours evenly, either sew with a needle and thread or use the glue gun to attach the leaves to the tree. To get a 3-D effect anchor each leaf just at the bottom edge, allowing the top part of the leaf to stand a little away from the back square. After applying approx. one third of the leaves, add in the blossom and then add the final leaves. Using a length of G and a yarn needle, work French knots (see page 127) in the centres of the white blossoms. Using a length of E, work some straight stitches (see page 126) around the bottom of the tree for grass.

For the summer tree:
Using a hot glue gun stick the tree stem in the centre of one of the A squares. Making sure to spread out the different sizes and different colours evenly, either sew with a needle and thread or use the glue gun to attach the leaves to the tree. To get a 3-D effect anchor each leaf just at the bottom edge, allowing the top part of the leaf to stand a little away from the back square. Using a double strand of J and a yarn needle, work French knots in among the leaves for the apples. Using a length of F work some straight stitches around the bottom of the tree for grass. Add a few apples around the bottom of the tree.

For the autumn tree:
Using a hot glue gun stick the tree stem in the centre of one of the A squares. Making sure to spread out the different sizes and different colours evenly, either sew with a needle and thread or use the glue gun to attach the leaves to the tree. To get a 3-D effect anchor each leaf just at the bottom edge, allowing the top part of the leaf to stand a little away from the back square. Using a length of M work some straight stitches around the bottom of the tree for grass. Add a few falling leaves dropping from the tree and around the bottom of the tree.

For the winter tree:
Using a hot glue gun stick the tree stem in the centre of one of the B squares. Sew the snow to the bottom of the square using the long yarn tail, taking it over the bottom of the tree trunk. Using H and a yarn needle work French knots all over the square and on top of the layer of snow. To finish, work in some French knots in D among the white and add some silver glitter glue to the tree trunk and branches.

Once all the squares are completed block (see page 123) to shape if needed.

When framing the squares use the hot glue gun to secure the squares to the back mount.

There can be nothing more special than a handmade Christmas card. This crochet picture version can even be framed once received and brought out on subsequent years as a Christmas decoration. The background square is worked in simple double crochet stitch in a cotton DK (light worsted) weight yarn and then the car and tree are made separately and stitched on afterwards. Again, only small quantities of yarn are needed so this project is perfect for using up any leftover yarn that you may have to hand.

christmas card

SKILL RATING ● ● ●

YARN AND MATERIALS

FOR THE BACKGROUND SQUARE:
Cascade Ultra Pima (100% cotton), DK (light worsted) weight, 200m (220yd) per 100g (3½oz) skein (hank)
- 1 skein of Gold 3747 (dark yellow) (A)

FOR THE CAR AND TREE:
Cascade Heritage (75% wool, 25% nylon), 4-ply (fingering) weight, 400m (437yd) per 100g (3½oz) skein (hank)
- Small amounts of:
  Red shade 5607 (B)
  White shade 5682 (C)
  Charcoal shade 5631 (dark grey) (D)
  Primavera shade 5659 (bright green) (E)
  Cedar Green shade 5684 (dark green) (F)

Rico Ricorumi Lamé (62% polyester, 38% nylon), DK (light worsted) weight, 50m (54yd) per 10g (⅜oz) ball
- 1 ball of Silver shade 001 (G)

12 x 12cm (4¾ x 4¾in) when folded tri-fold card blank, aperture size 9 x 9cm (3½ x 3½in)

Small twig for tree trunk

Silver glitter glue

Small piece of string or yarn

HOOK AND EQUIPMENT

2.5mm (US B-1 to C-2) crochet hook

3mm (US D) crochet hook

Stitch marker

Yarn needle

Sewing needle and thread

Hot glue gun

TENSION (GAUGE)

25 sts x 28 rows = 10 x 10cm (4 x 4in) working double crochet using a 3mm (US D) crochet hook and Cascade Ultra Pima.

FINISHED MEASUREMENTS

Finished card: 12 x 12cm (4¾ x 4¾in)
Finished square approx. 9.5 x 9.5cm (3¾ x 3¾in)

ABBREVIATIONS
See page 127.

KEY POINTS

For a neat bottom edge to each square see page 118 for details of working into the back bump of the starting chain.

As the crochet square is going to be behind the aperture in the card there will be no need to work a finishing border.

I used two strands of 4-ply (fingering) held together when making the car and the tree so one strand of DK (light worsted) weight would work equally as well. For the tree, I used strands of different colour greens to add extra definition but one colour would work equally well.

BACKGROUND SQUARE

Using a 3mm (US D) hook and A, ch24.
Row 1: Starting in second ch from hook, 1dc in back bump of each ch to end, turn. (*23 sts*)
Row 2: Ch1 (does not count as st), 1dc in each st to end, turn.
Rows 3–22: Rep Row 2.
Fasten off and sew in ends (see page 123).

CAR BODY

Using a 2.5mm (US B-1 to C-2) hook and two strands of B held together, ch18.
Row 1: Starting in second ch from hook, 1dc in back bump of each ch to end, turn. (*17 sts*)
Row 2: Ch1 (does not count as st throughout), dc2tog, 1dc in each st to end, turn. (*16 sts*)
Row 3: Ch1, 1dc in each st to last 2 sts, dc2tog, turn. (*15 sts*)
Row 4: Ch1, 1dc in each st to last 2 sts, dc2tog, turn. (*14 sts*)
Row 5: Ch1, 1dc in each st to last 2 sts, dc2tog, turn. (*13 sts*)
Fasten off and sew in ends.

Roof

With RS facing, count in 5 sts from top right-hand corner, join two strands of B held together in next st with a sl st, ch17.
Starting in second ch from hook, 1dc in each ch back to original st on top edge, sew in ends where ch starts.
Making sure that roof piece is not twisted, sew other end to back edge of car.

Edging
With RS facing and two strands of B held together, starting at bottom of roof at back of car, 1dc in each st and 2dc in any sts on a curve, all around car and over top of roof to beg of round, sl st in beg of round to join. Fasten off and sew in ends.

WHEELS
Using a 2.5mm (US B-1 to C-2) hook and two strands of C held together, make a magic ring.
Round 1: 6dc into ring, sl st to join. (*6 sts*)
Fasten off C.
Round 2: Join two strands of D held together with a sl st and 2dc in same st, 2dc in each st around, sl st in beg of round to join. (*12 sts*)
Fasten off D and sew in ends.

CHRISTMAS TREE
Worked in continuous rounds.
Using a 2.5mm (US B-1 to C-2) hook and one strand of E and one strand of F held together, make a magic ring.
Round 1: 4dc into ring.
Round 2: [1dc in next st, 2dc in next st] twice, PM for beg of round. (*6 sts*)
Round 3: [1dc in each of next 2 sts, 2dc in next st] twice. (*8 sts*)
Round 4: 1dc in each st.
Round 5: [1dc in each of next 3 sts, 2dc in next st] twice. (*10 sts*)
Round 6: 1dc in each st.
Round 7: [1dc in each of next 2 sts, 2dc in next st] 3 times, 1dc in last st. (*13 sts*)
Round 8: [1dc in each of next 3 sts, 2dc in next st] 3 times, 1dc in last st. (*16 sts*)
Round 9: [1dc in each of next 4 sts, 2dc in next st] 3 times, 1dc in last st. (*19 sts*)
Round 10: 1dc in each st.
Round 11: [1 dc in each of next 2 sts, 2dc in next st] 6 times, 1dc in last st. (*25 sts*)
Round 12: 1dc in each st.
Round 13: [1dc in each of next 5 sts, 2dc in next st] 4 times, 1dc in last st. (*29 sts*)
Fasten off and sew in ends.

FINISHING
Place the background square inside the card mount. To allow room for the tree, place the car in position, very slightly over to the right rather than completely central, and sew in place with a sewing needle and thread. Using a length of B and a yarn needle, sew a couple of straight stitches (see page 126) from the underside of the roof down to the top edge of the car for the window divider. Stitch a square to indicate the car door. Using a length of D and a yarn needle, sew a couple of short straight stitches for the steering wheel and the exhaust, and work a French knot (see page 127) for a door handle. Sew the wheels in place with a sewing needle and thread.

Using G work a few French knots onto the tree. Gently shape the tree so that the back is slightly pushed in towards the centre to create a 3-D shape. Use a hot glue gun to stick the tree trunk inside the tree. Add a little glitter glue to the trunk.

Position the tree on top of the car and, using a yarn needle and either a piece of string or yarn, stitch around the tree to tie it to the roof of the car. Using a sewing needle and thread sew the tree in place.

To finish, use C and a yarn needle to sew snow onto the square using French knots.

Add a few French knots in G among the snow and then a few along the ground underneath the car.

Finally, use a hot glue gun to stick the crochet square securely into the card mount.

how to use and display the picture squares

Framed pictures and collages
Many of the squares in this book, such as the wedding day or new baby squares, can be made and framed as individual pictures to serve as a permanent memory of a special occasion.

As most of the squares feature a slightly three-dimensional aspect the best frames to use are box frames, as these allow for the extra depth that the squares will have.

As shown with the Seasonal tree picture (see page 110), several picture squares mounted together in one collage box frame also work well. For this a 30cm (12in) square box frame with four 10 x 10cm (4 x 4in) mounts is a good size fit. Squares that could also work well for this are the four different seasonal wreaths, or a selection of the different Christmas squares.

Greetings cards
Any of the squares in this book lend themselves perfectly to being made into greetings cards, whether for a birthday, wedding, new home, Valentine, Diwali or Easter. Each individual square can be stuck onto a tri-fold card blank and sent through the post. Tri-fold card blanks are readily available from craft shops or online and usually come with an envelope.

I found the best way to attach the squares to the card is to use a hot glue gun as this gives a really good bond to hold the square in place.

When making the squares for cards some of the designs, such as the bunch of roses, the heart and the trees from the Seasonal tree picture (see page 110) could also double up as thank you cards.

Garlands
As with the Autumn Garland (see page 104) in the projects section, the squares also work well made into a crocheted garland. This is such a simple way to display your work, as the squares can be stitched onto a length of cord, ribbon or string.

The Christmas squares are designed to sit well together, and you could make them into Christmas bunting to bring out each year. Why not make the perfect personalised wedding garland with the two wedding squares, the seasonal wreath for the time of year the wedding falls in, a bunch of roses in the wedding colour scheme and a square with balloons to match. To stretch the bunting out if needed you can alternate the picture squares with plain squares, worked to the same pattern as the picture square bases.

Blankets and cushions
Another way that the squares can be used is in larger crocheted blanket and cushion projects. For example, if you have worked a plain crochet baby blanket but wish to personalise it a little, you could stitch either of the new baby squares onto the main blanket as a corner motif.

The Christmas squares or the Easter and Spring squares (which don't have delicate or fragile elements such as the twigs in the Easter Nest) could also be made and then worked into a patchwork cushion or blanket. For the extra squares, use any of the colours from the picture squares to keep the continuity, and work the extra squares to the same pattern as the picture square bases. They will fit together neatly once joined, either by stitching or crocheting the seams together (see page 124).

techniques

This section guides you through all the crochet and finishing techniques that you will need to make the squares and projects in this book.

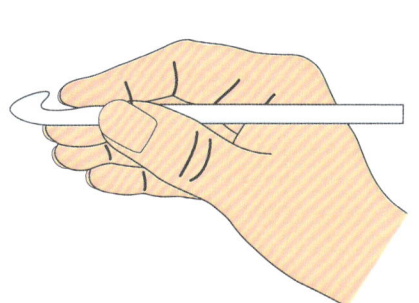
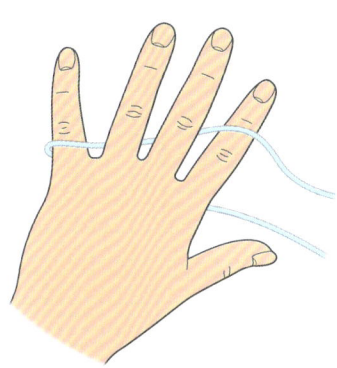
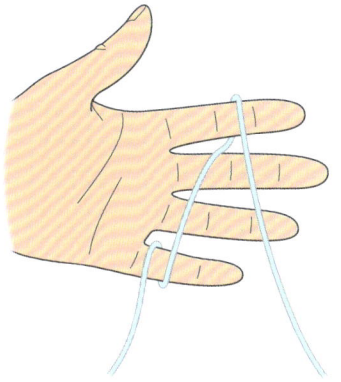

Holding the hook
Pick up your hook as though you are picking up a pen or pencil. Keeping the hook held loosely between your fingers and thumb, turn your hand so that the palm is facing up and the hook is balanced in your hand and resting in the space between your index finger and your thumb.

You can also hold the hook like a knife – this may be easier if you are working with a large hook or with chunky (bulky) yarn. Choose the method that you find most comfortable.

Holding the yarn
1 Pick up the yarn with your little finger in the opposite hand to your hook, with your palm facing upwards and with the short end in front. Turn your hand to face downwards, with the yarn on top of your index finger and under the other two fingers and wrapped right around the little finger, as shown above.

2 Turn your hand to face you, ready to hold the work in your middle finger and thumb. Keeping your index finger only at a slight curve, hold the work or the slip knot using the same hand, between your middle finger and your thumb and just below the crochet hook and loop/s on the hook.

Holding the hook and yarn while crocheting
Keep your index finger, with the yarn draped over it, at a slight curve, and hold your work (or the slip knot) using the same hand, between your middle finger and your thumb and just below the crochet hook and loop/s on the hook.

As you draw the loop through the hook release the yarn on the index finger to allow the loop to stay loose on the hook. If you tense your index finger, the yarn will become too tight and pull the loop on the hook too tight for you to draw the yarn through.

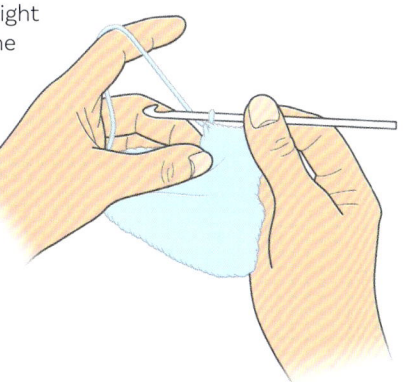

Holding the hook and yarn for left-handers
Some left-handers learn to crochet like right-handers, but others learn with everything reversed – with the hook in the left hand and the yarn in the right.

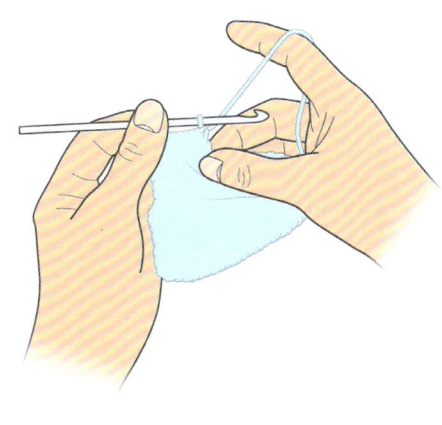

Making a slip knot

The simplest way is to make a circle with the yarn, so that the loop is facing downwards.

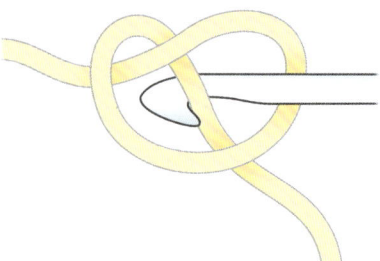

1 In one hand hold the circle at the top where the yarn crosses, and let the tail drop down at the back so that it falls across the centre of the loop. With your free hand or the tip of a crochet hook, pull a loop through the circle.

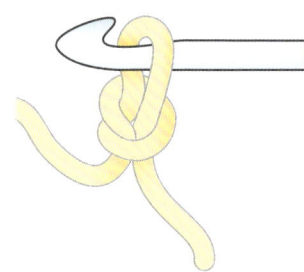

2 Put the hook into the loop and pull gently so that it forms a loose loop on the hook.

Yarn round hook (yrh)

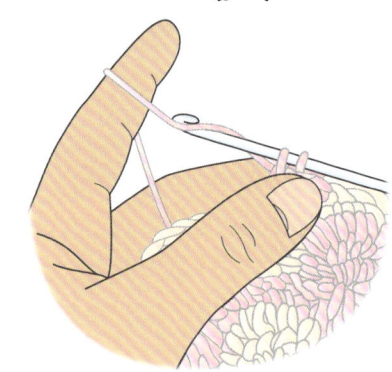

To create a stitch, catch the yarn from behind with the hook pointing upwards. As you gently pull the yarn through the loop on the hook, turn the hook so it faces downwards and slide the yarn through the loop. The loop on the hook should be kept loose enough for the hook to slide through easily.

Chain (ch)

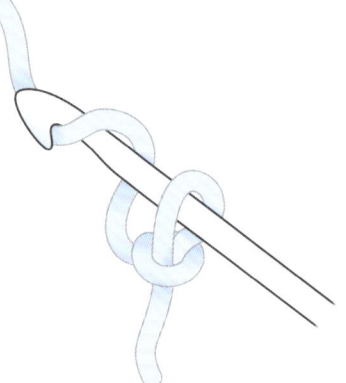

1 Using the hook, wrap the yarn round the hook ready to pull it through the loop on the hook.

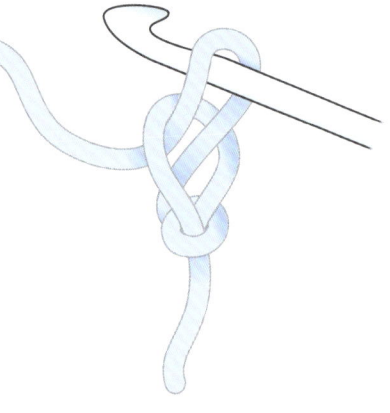

2 Pull through, creating a new loop on the hook. Continue in this way to create a chain of the required length.

Working into a foundation chain

Working into the front of the foundation chain

The front of the chain (the right side) is the smooth side: each chain makes a little 'V', as shown here. To make the first stitch into your foundation chain, using the point of the tip of the hook and with the hook tilted slightly sideways, insert the hook into the middle of the chain, picking up the loop at the top of the chain.

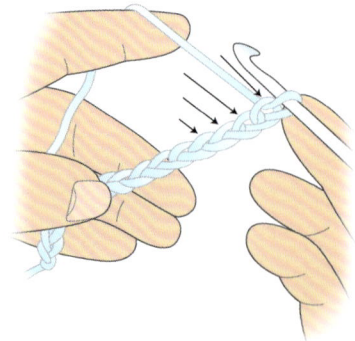

Working into the back of the foundation chain

The back of the chain (the wrong side) is more bumpy, with little ridges. To make the first stitch into the back of the foundation chain, using the point of the tip of the hook and with the hook tilted slightly sideways, insert the hook into the bump at the back of the chain.

Chain ring

If you are crocheting a round shape, one way of starting off is by crocheting a number of chains following the instructions in your pattern, and then joining them into a circle.

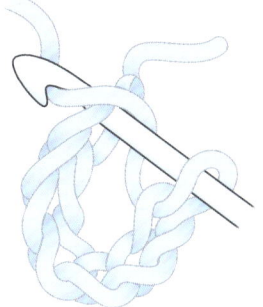

1 To join the chain into a circle, insert the crochet hook into the first chain that you made (not into the slip knot), yarn round hook.

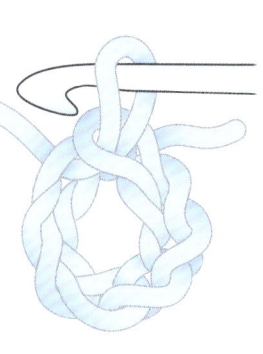

2 Pull the yarn through the chain and through the loop on your hook at the same time, thereby creating a slip stitch and forming a circle. You now have a chain ring ready to work stitches into as instructed in the pattern.

Magic ring

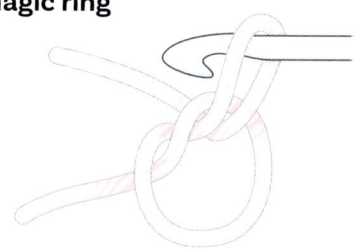

This is a useful starting technique if you do not want a visible hole in the centre of your round. Loop the yarn around your finger, insert the hook through the ring, yarn round hook, pull through the ring to make the first chain. Work the number of stitches required into the ring and then pull the end to tighten the centre ring and close the hole.

Slip stitch (sl st)

A slip stitch doesn't create any height and is often used as the last stitch to create a smooth and even round or row.

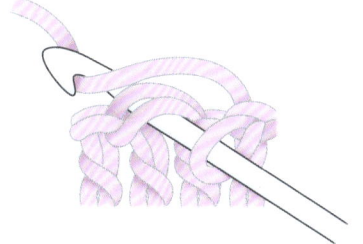

1 To make a slip stitch: first put the hook through the work, yarn round hook.

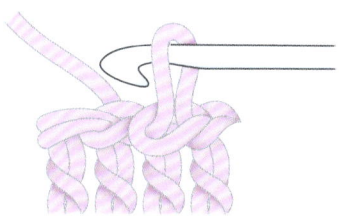

2 Pull the yarn through both the work and through the loop on the hook at the same time, so you will have 1 loop on the hook.

Making rounds

When working in rounds the work is not turned, so you are always working from one side. Depending on the pattern you are working, a 'round' can be square. Start each round by making one or more chains to create the height you need for the stitch you are working:

Double crochet = 1 chain
Half treble crochet = 2 chains
Treble crochet = 3 chains
Double treble = 4 chains

Work the required stitches to complete the round. At the end of the round, slip stitch into the top of the chain to close the round.

Continuous spiral

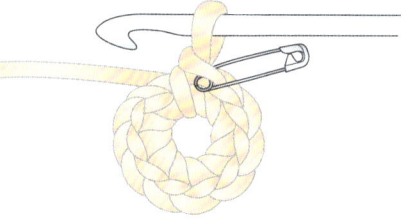

If you work in a spiral you do not need a turning chain. After completing the base ring, place a stitch marker in the first stitch and then continue to crochet around. When you have made a round and reached the point where the stitch marker is, work this stitch, take out the stitch marker from the previous round and put it back into the first stitch of the new round. A safety pin or piece of yarn in a contrasting colour makes a good stitch marker.

Making rows

When making straight rows you turn the work at the end of each row and make a turning chain to create the height you need for the stitch you are working with, as for making rounds.

Double crochet = 1 chain
Half treble crochet = 2 chains
Treble crochet = 3 chains
Double treble = 4 chains

Working into top of stitch

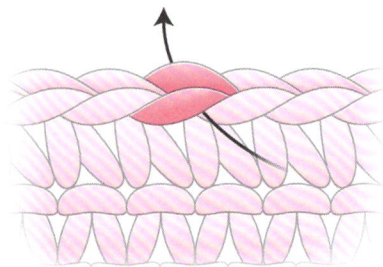

Unless otherwise directed, always insert the hook under both of the two loops on top of the stitch – this is the standard technique.

Working into front loop of stitch (FLO)

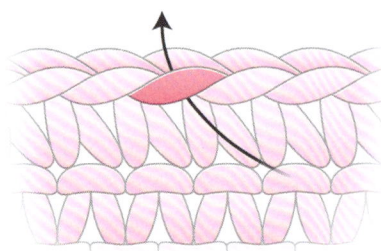

To work into the front loop of a stitch, pick up the front loop from underneath at the front of the work.

Working into back loop of stitch (BLO)

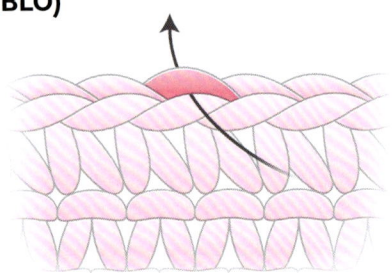

To work into the back loop of the stitch, insert the hook between the front and the back loop, picking up the back loop from the front of the work.

Double crochet (dc)

1 Insert the hook into your work, yarn round hook and pull the yarn through the work only. You will then have 2 loops on the hook.

2 Yarn round hook again and pull through the 2 loops on the hook. You will then have 1 loop on the hook.

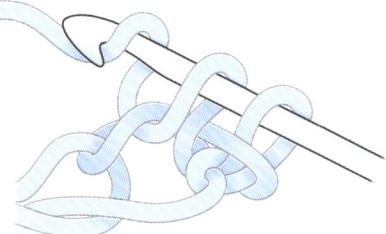

Half treble crochet (htr)

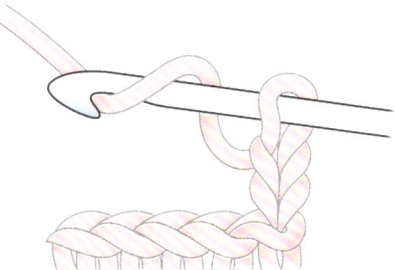

1 Before inserting the hook into the work, wrap the yarn round the hook and put the hook through the work with the yarn wrapped around.

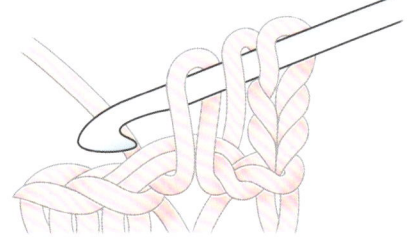

2 Yarn round hook again and pull through the first loop on the hook. You now have 3 loops on the hook.

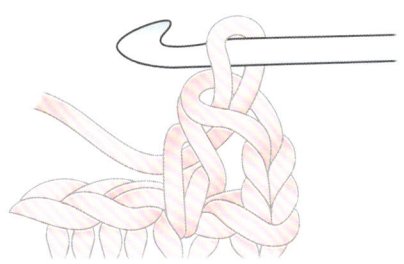

3 Yarn round hook and pull the yarn through all 3 loops. You will be left with 1 loop on the hook.

Treble crochet (tr)

 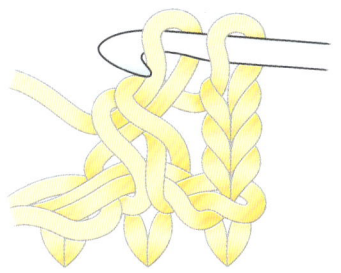 

1 Before inserting the hook into the work, wrap the yarn round the hook. Put the hook through the work with the yarn wrapped around, yarn round hook again and pull through the first loop on the hook. You now have 3 loops on the hook.

2 Yarn round hook again, pull the yarn through the first 2 loops on the hook. You now have 2 loops on the hook.

3 Pull the yarn through 2 loops again. You will be left with 1 loop on the hook.

Double treble crochet (dtr)

Yarn round hook twice, insert the hook into the stitch, yarn round hook, pull a loop through (4 loops on hook), yarn round hook, pull the yarn through 2 stitches (3 loops on hook), yarn round hook, pull a loop through the next 2 stitches (2 loops on hook), yarn round hook, pull a loop through the last 2 stitches. You will be left with 1 loop on the hook.

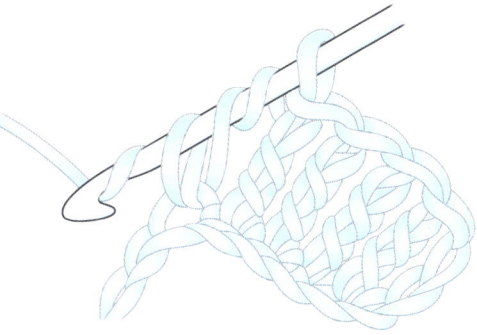

Increasing

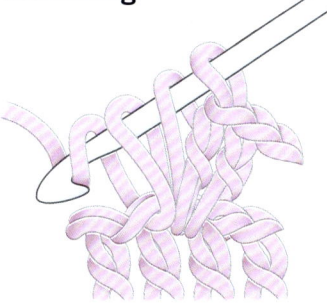

Make two or three stitches into one stitch or space from the previous row. The illustration shows a treble crochet increase being made.

Decreasing

You can decrease by either missing the next stitch and continuing to crochet, or by crocheting two or more stitches together. The basic technique for crocheting stitches together is the same, no matter which stitch you are using. The following example shows dc2tog.

Double crochet two stitches together (dc2tog)

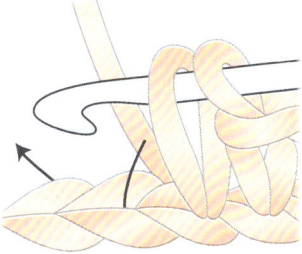 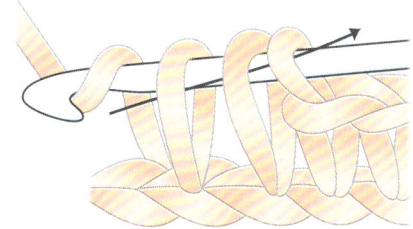

1 Insert the hook into your work, yarn round hook and pull the yarn through the work (2 loops on hook). Insert the hook in next stitch, yarn round hook and pull the yarn through.

2 Yarn round hook again and pull through all 3 loops on the hook. You will then have 1 loop on the hook.

Enclosing a yarn tail

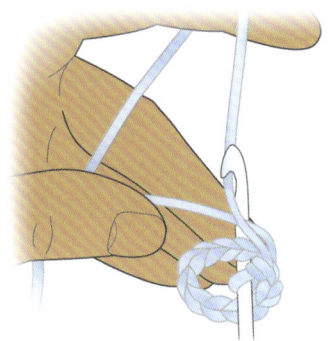

You may find that the yarn tail gets in the way as you work; you can enclose this into the stitches as you go by placing the tail at the back as you wrap the yarn. This also saves having to sew this tail end in later.

Joining yarn with a slip stitch

You can use this technique when changing colour, or when joining in a new ball of yarn as one runs out.

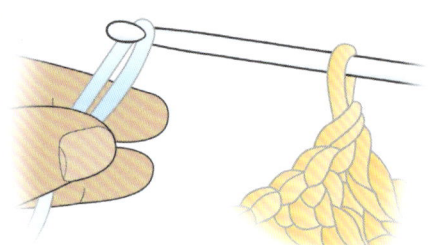

1 Keep the loop of the old yarn on the hook. Drop the tail and catch a loop of the strand of the new yarn with the crochet hook.

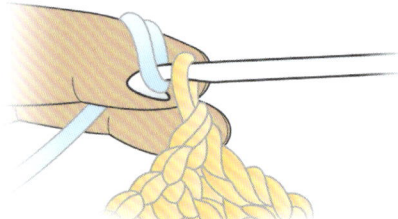

2 Draw the new yarn through the loop on the hook, keeping the old loop drawn tight and continue as instructed in the pattern.

Changing colour in the middle of a row or round or on last yarn round hook

This method can be used to create a neat colour join in the middle of a row or round, or on the last yarn round hook (yrh).

Joining a new colour into double crochet

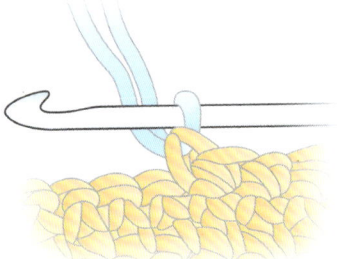

1 Make a double crochet stitch (see page 120), but do not draw the final loop through, so there are 2 loops on the hook. Drop the old yarn, catch the new yarn with the hook and draw it through both loops to complete the stitch and join in the new colour at the same time.

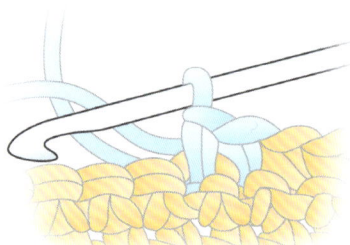

2 Continue to crochet with the new yarn. Cut the old yarn leaving a 15cm (6in) tail and weave the tail in (see right) after working a row, or once the work is complete.

Working over yarn along a row

Working over the yarn along a row involves carrying one or more additional colours through the work until you are ready to use them. It's the crochet equivalent of Fair Isle or stranding in knitting, but with the bonus that the second colour is not visible at the back of the work – it is fully enclosed in the stitches of the first colour.

Joining a new colour into double crochet

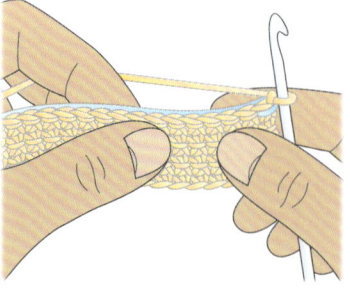

1 Hold the second colour yarn along the top of the stitches from the previous row. You can do this from the beginning of a row, or join it a few stitches before you need to start using it, if it is only going to be used for a small area.

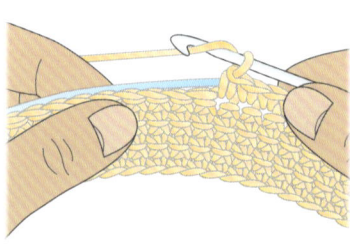

2 Work stitches in the normal way in the first colour, but going over the second colour and ensuring it is 'trapped' within the stitches. Continue working in this way, carrying the second colour until you are ready to work a stitch in it.

122 techniques

Changing colour in double crochet

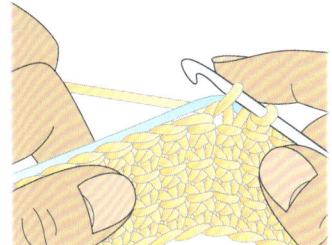
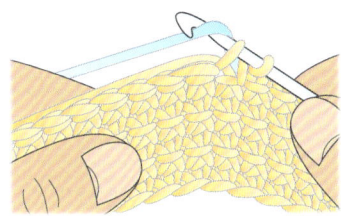
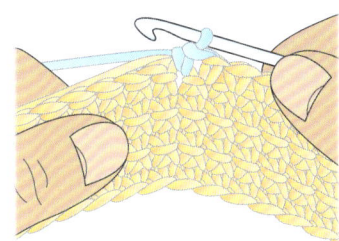

1 With the first colour, pull the yarn through the next stitch, yarn over and pull through.

2 Using the second colour, yarn over hook.

3 Pull the new colour yarn through both loops on the hook to complete the stitch and change to the new colour. Continue in the second colour, working over the first colour.

Turning at the end of a row

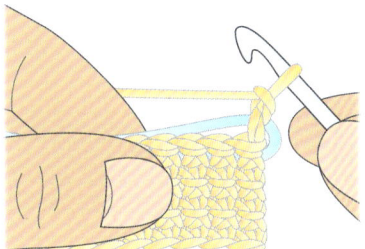
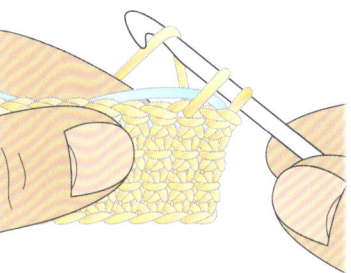

1 With the working colour, make the appropriate length turning chain. Pull the second yarn up, holding it tight along the top of your work. Work the next stitch over the second yarn, catching it behind the piece.

2 Continue to work over the second yarn as shown.

Fastening off

When you have finished crocheting, you need to fasten off the stitches to stop all your work unravelling.

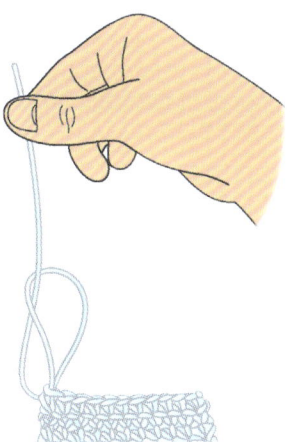

Draw up the final loop of the last stitch to make it bigger. Cut the yarn, leaving a tail of approximately 10cm (4in) – unless a longer end is needed for sewing up. Pull the tail all the way through the loop and pull the loop up tightly.

Sewing in yarn ends

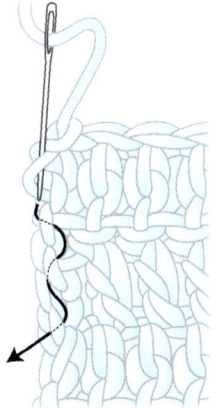

It is important to sew in the tail ends of the yarn so that they are secure and your crochet won't unravel. Thread a yarn needle with the tail end of yarn. On the wrong side, take the needle through the crochet one stitch down on the edge, then take it through the stitches, working in a gentle zigzag. Work through four or five stitches then return in the opposite direction. Remove the needle, pull the crochet gently to stretch it and trim the end.

Blocking

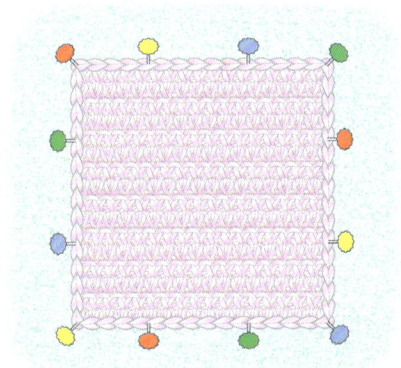

Crochet can tend to curl, so to make flat pieces stay flat you may need to block them. Pin the piece out to the correct size and shape on an ironing board or some soft foam mats (such as the ones sold as children's play mats). Spray the crochet with water and leave it to dry completely before unpinning and removing from the board or mats.

Joining squares together

Making a double crochet seam or slip stitch seam

With a double crochet seam you join two pieces together using a crochet hook and working a double crochet stitch through both pieces, instead of sewing them together with a tail of yarn and a yarn sewing needle. This makes a quick and strong seam and gives a slightly raised finish to the edging. For a less raised seam, follow the same basic technique, but work each stitch in slip stitch rather than double crochet.

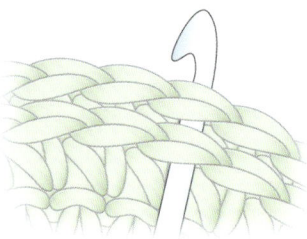
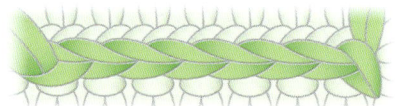
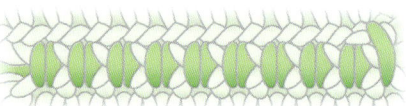

1 Start by lining up the two pieces with wrong sides together. Insert the hook in the top 2 loops of the stitch of the first piece, then into the corresponding stitch on the second piece.

2 Complete the double crochet stitch as normal and continue on the next stitches as directed in the pattern. This gives a raised effect if the double crochet stitches are made on the right side of the work.

3 You can work with the wrong side of the work facing (with the pieces right side facing) if you don't want this effect and it still creates a good strong join.

Making an oversewn seam

An oversewn join gives a nice flat seam and is the simplest and most common joining technique.

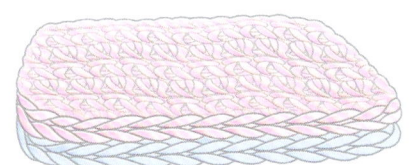
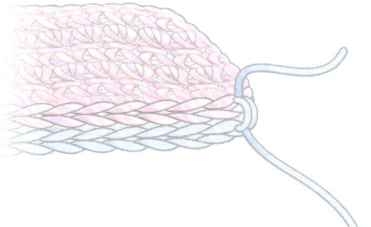
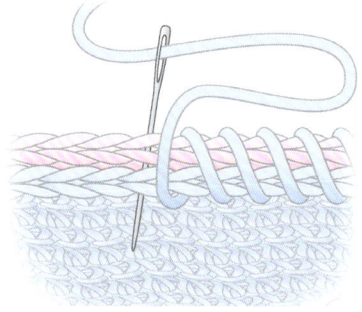

1 Thread a yarn sewing needle with the yarn you're using in the project. Place the pieces to be joined with right sides together.

2 Insert the needle in one corner in the top loops of the stitches of both pieces and pull up the yarn, leaving a tail of about 5cm (2in). Go into the same place with the needle and pull up the yarn again; repeat two or three times to secure the yarn at the start of the seam.

3 Join the pieces together by taking the needle through the loops at the top of corresponding stitches on each piece to the end. Fasten off the yarn at the end, as in step 2.

Crab stitch

This is simply double crochet worked backwards to give a twisted edge. Crab stitch spreads the edge slightly, so there's no need to crease to turn a corner. If a straight edge flutes, either miss the occasional stitch or use a smaller hook.

Do not turn the work at the end of the last row. Insert the hook in the last stitch to the right, yarn round hook and pull through to make two loops twisted on the hook. Yarn round hook again and pull through making one loop on the hook. Repeat in the stitches along the edge or in row ends if necessary.

Bobble

Bobbles are created when working on wrong-side rows and the bobble is then pushed out towards the right-side row. This is a four-treble cluster bobble (4trCL), and it shows the general technique for making bobbles. The bobbles in the patterns are worked in slightly different ways – make sure you follow the exact instructions in the pattern.

1 Yarn round hook and then insert the hook in the stitch, yarn round hook and pull the yarn through the work.

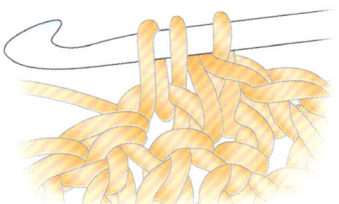

2 Yarn round hook and pull the yarn through the first 2 loops on the hook (2 loops on hook).

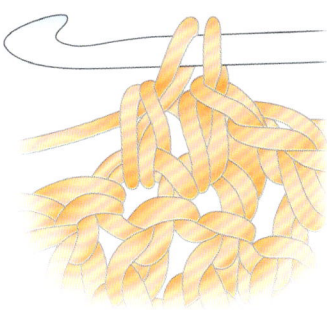

3 Repeat steps 1 and 2 three more times in the same stitch, yarn round hook and pull through all 5 loops on the hook.

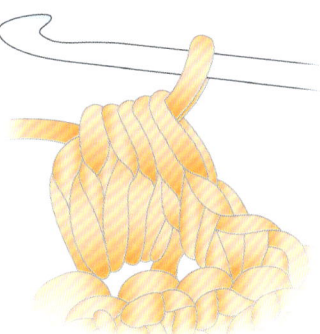

4 You can also make 1 chain to complete the bobble.

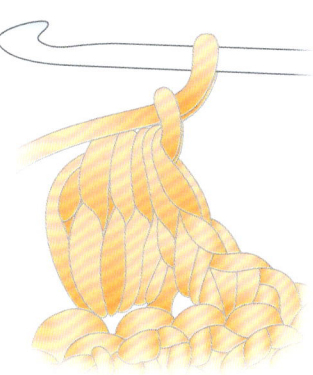

Picots

A picot is a little bobble texture that is often used to create decorative little points along the outer edge of an edging. This sample shows how to make a 3ch-picot, but follow the instructions in the pattern for the number of chains to make.

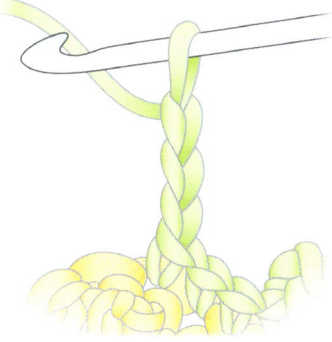

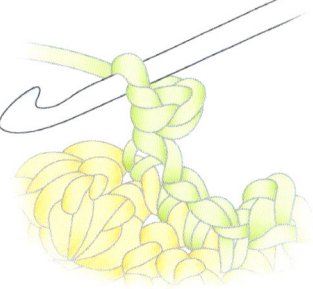

1 Make 14ch.
Row 1: 1dc in second ch from hook, 1dc in each ch to end.
Row 2: 1ch, 1dc in each of next 2 sts, 3tr in next st, *1dc in each of the next 3 sts, 3tr in next st, rep from * twice more, 2dc in each of last 2 sts.
Row 3 (picot row): 1ch, 1dc in each of next 2 dc, 1dc in top of next tr, *3ch,

2 Sl st in third ch from hook (one picot made), 1dc in top of next tr.

3 Rep from * once more, 3ch, sl st in third ch from hook (picot made)**, 1dc in each of next 3 dc, 1dc in top of next tr, rep from * ending last rep at **, 1dc in each of last two dc.

Surface crochet

Surface crochet is a simple way to add extra decoration to a finished item, working slip stitches over the surface of the fabric.

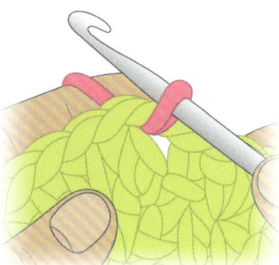 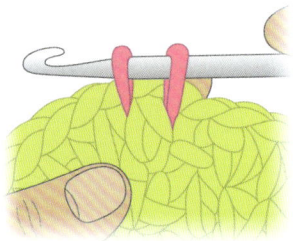 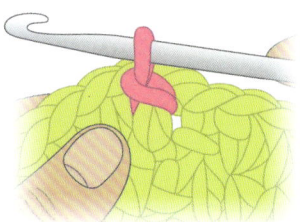

1 Using a contrast yarn, make a slip knot (see page 118). Holding the yarn with the slip knot behind the work and the hook in front, insert the hook between two stitches from front to the back and catch the slip knot behind the work with the hook. Draw the slip knot back through, so there is 1 loop on the hook at the front of the work.

2 Insert the hook between the next 2 stitches, yarn round hook and draw a loop through to the front. You will now have 2 loops on the hook.

3 Pull the first loop on the hook through the second loop to complete the first slip stitch on the surface of the work. Repeat steps 2 and 3 to make the next slip stitch. To join two ends with an invisible join, cut the yarn and thread onto a yarn needle. Insert the needle up through the last stitch, into the first stitch as if you were crocheting it, then into the back loop of the previous stitch. Fasten off on the wrong side.

Double crochet border

Adding an edging neatens up the sides of crochet, and it can also be used to make a frame in a contrasting colour to create a good effect. A double crochet border usually starts at a corner and you will be instructed in the pattern where to join the yarn. It's usually worked on the right side of the work. There are usually 2 or 3 stitches made in the corner to create the corner shape, then you make double crochet stitches along the edge to the next corner, and so on until you have worked around the whole piece. When you are working along the sides it's not always obvious where to place your hook or how to place the stitches evenly. A good method is to use either pin or stitch markers, placing them at the halfway and quarter points, then divide the number of stitches required along the edge into four so that as you get to each marker you know you have placed the stitches evenly. At the end of the round, join the first and last stitches with a slip stitch.

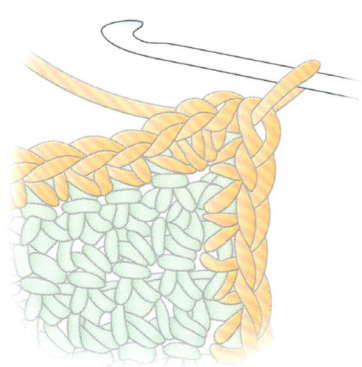

Embroidery

These decorative hand-sewing techniques are used to add details to some of the projects.

Running stitch

Bring the needle to the surface of the fabric and take it back down to the left of the entry point, to create a straight stitch. Bring the needle back to the surface a stitch length away from the last stitch and return through the fabric as before. Continue to create stitches of equal length.

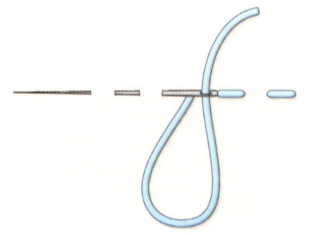

Straight stitch

Bring the needle through to the surface of the fabric and then take it back down to create a small straight stitch. These can be worked at different lengths and angles to create a variety of effects.

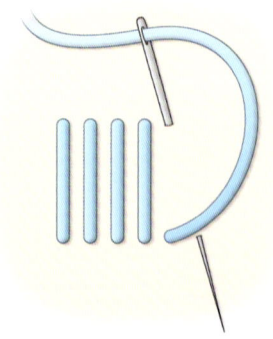

Satin stitch

Bring the needle up to the surface of the fabric, then take it back down at the selected point, drawing the yarn flush against the fabric. Bring the needle back up and down again next to the previous stitch. Continue in this manner, drawing the yarn smoothly against the surface of the fabric to fill the chosen area. The stitches should be close together, with no fabric visible in between them. They can be worked to add a solid effect, such as the centre of a flower, in your finished project.

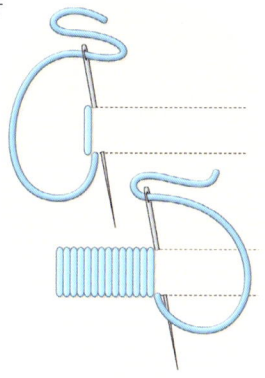

French knots

Bring the needle up to the surface at the position of the knot. Holding the embroidery thread (floss) taut, wrap it two or three times around the tip of the needle. Continue holding the embroidery thread under tension as you pass the needle back down through the fabric close to the entry point. The embroidery thread will pull through the wraps and they will form a knot that sits on the surface of the fabric.

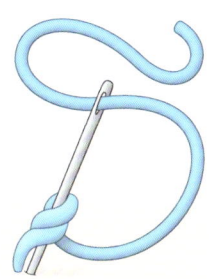

Abbreviations

approx.	approximately
beg	beginning
BLO	back loop only
ch	chain
cont	continu(e)ing
dc	double crochet
dc2tog	double crochet 2 stitches together
dtr	double treble
FLO	front loop only
htr	half treble
MB	make bobble
PM	place marker
rem	remain(ing)
rep	repeat
RS	right side
sl st	slip stitch
sp(s)	space(s)
tog	together
tr	treble
WS	wrong side
yrh	yarn round hook
*	repeat sequence from * number of times stated
( )	work stitches inside brackets all into same stitch or space stated
[ ]	work sequence inside square brackets number of times stated

Suppliers

We cannot cover all stockists here, so please explore the local yarn shops and online retailers in your own country. If you wish to substitute a different yarn for the one recommended in the pattern, try the Yarnsub website for suggestions: www.yarnsub.com.

Etsy
Square aperture card blanks and 3-D box photo frames
I used the square aperture tri-fold card blanks (5-pack, 16 colours or mixed pack, 12cm/4¾in square card with 9cm/3½in window) from HandycraftTime, and a 3-D box photo frame (12.5cm/5in square in Natural) from NIFrames Direct.

UK
LoveCrafts
Online sales
www.lovecrafts.com

Wool
Yarn, hooks
Store in Bath
+44 (0)1225 469144
www.woolbath.co.uk

Wool Warehouse
Online sales
www.woolwarehouse.co.uk

VV Rouleaux
Ribbons and rope cord
Store in London
+44 (0)20 7627 4455
www.vvrouleaux.com

Laughing Hens
Online sales
Tel: +44 (0)1829 740903
www.laughinghens.com

John Lewis
Yarns and craft supplies
Telephone numbers of stores on website
www.johnlewis.com

Hobbycraft
Yarns and craft supplies
www.hobbycraft.co.uk

USA
LoveCrafts
Online sales
www.lovecrafts.com

Knitting Fever Inc.
www.knittingfever.com

WEBS
www.yarn.com

Michaels
Craft supplies
www.michaels.com

Australia
Black Sheep Wool 'n' Wares
Retail store and online
Tel: +61 (0)2 6779 1196
www.blacksheepwool.com.au

Sunspun
Retail store in Canterbury, Victoria and online
Tel: +61 (0)3 9830 1609
www.sunspun.com.au

Crochet stitch conversion chart

Crochet stitches are worked in the same way in both the UK and the USA, but the stitch names are not the same and identical names are used for different stitches. Below is a list of the UK terms used in this book, and the equivalent US terms.

UK TERM	US TERM
double crochet (dc)	single crochet (sc)
half treble (htr)	half double crochet (hdc)
treble (tr)	double crochet (dc)
double treble (dtr)	treble (tr)
tension	gauge
yarn round hook (yrh)	yarn over hook (yoh)

Acknowledgements

Thank you to the amazing team at CICO Books and MAKEetc, who have once again allowed me to create a crochet book that I couldn't be prouder of. I am so grateful for their faith in me and for allowing me to make my crochet dreams become reality. It is always so exciting when the first photos start to come back through showing my designs so beautifully styled and photographed.

index

abbreviations 127
Autumn Garland 104-9
Autumn Hedgehog with Toadstool Umbrella 23-5
Autumn Wreath 20-2

Baby's Pram 54-6
bag, Bobbly Grab 95-7
Birthday Cupcake 52-3
Birthday Present 50-1
blankets 116
　Gingham Baby 90-1
　Tutti-Fruitti 84-6
blocking 5, 123
bobbles 125
Bobbly Grab Bag 95-7

chain stitch 118
changing colour 122-3
Chequered Place Mats and Coasters 98-100
Christmas Card 113-15
Christmas Letter Box and Presents 79-81
Christmas Tree 76-8
Christmas Wreath 74-5
Chunky Bobbly Cushions 92-4
coasters, Chequered 98-100
collages 116
continuous spiral 119
conversion charts 127
crab stitch 124
crochet techniques 117-27
cushions 116
　Chunky Bobbly 92-4

Daisy-and-Dot Hot Water Bottle Cover 101-3
decreasing 121
displaying picture squares 116

Diwali Candle 68-70
double crochet 120
double crochet border 126
double treble crochet 121

Easter Nest 65-7
Easter Rabbit 62-4
embroidery 126-7

fastening off 123
foundation chain, working into 119
framed pictures 116
　Seasonal Tree Picture 110-12
French knots 127

garlands 116
　Autumn Garland 104-9
Gingham Baby Blanket 90-1
greeting cards 116
　Christmas Card 113-15

half treble crochet 120
Hanukkah Candelabra 71-3
hook, holding 117
hot water bottle cover, Daisy-and-Dot 101-3

increasing 121

magic ring 119
Mistletoe Sprig 26-8
motifs, adding 5

New Baby in a Basket 57-9
New Home Cottage Scene 45-7
New Home Front Door 48-9

oversewn seams 124

picots 125
place mats, Chequered 98-100

rounds 119
rows 119
running stitch 126

satin stitch 127
seams 124
Seasonal Tree Picture 110-12
slip knots 118
slip stitch 119, 122
spiral, continuous 119
Spring Blossom Wreath 8-10
Spring Snowdrops 11-13
Square Tissue Box Cover 87-9
straight stitch 126
Summer Beehive and Foxgloves 14-16
Summer Meadow 17-19
surface crochet 126

techniques 117-27
tension 5
Tissue Box Cover, Square 87-9
treble crochet 121
Tutti-fruitti Blanket 84-6

Valentine's Bouquet 40-1
Valentine's Heart 42-4

weaving in 123
Wedding Cake 37-9
Wedding Car 34-6
Winter Penguin 29-31
working into stitches 120
working over yarn 122

yarn 4
　enclosing tails 122
　holding 117
　joining 122
yarn round hook 119